GERRY MAND ERING TEXAS

STEVE BICKERSTAFF

GERRY
MAND
ERING
TEXAS

EDITED BY C. ROBERT HEATH

TEXAS TECH UNIVERSITY PRESS

This book is typeset in Crimson Text. The paper used in this book meets the minimum requirements of ANSI/NISO Z39.48-1992 (R1997). ∞

Designed by Hannah Gaskamp
Cover image used with permission from The Texas General Land Office

Library of Congress Control Number: 2020942538

ISBN 978-1-68283-073-4 (paperback)

Printed in the United States of America
20 21 22 23 24 25 26 27 28 / 9 8 7 6 5 4 3 2 1

Texas Tech University Press
Box 41037
Lubbock, Texas 79409-1037 USA
800.832.4042
ttup@ttu.edu
www.ttupress.org

CONTENTS

ILLUSTRATIONS AND MAPS

All congressional maps courtesy of the Texas Legislative Council

FOREWORD

STEVE BICKERSTAFF, THE AUTHOR OF this book, was my friend. For eighteen years he was my law partner. Although the law practice (currently Bickerstaff Heath Delgado Acosta LLP) that the two of us founded in 1980 has grown and undergone various name changes both before and after his retirement in 1998, his surname has always been first among the names that identify the firm.

Not long after finishing revisions on this book, Steve unexpectedly died. While there remained some minor editing to complete, the product is wholly Steve's. There was no one better able to write this story. To a large extent, Texas redistricting was Steve's life. This is not to diminish the other important aspects of his life—his family, his career, his love of travel and the outdoors—or to suggest that it held a place superior to that of other personal and professional facets of his being. Rather, the story of Texas redistricting and Steve's professional life overlapped substantially across a long and meaningful period. It is doubtful that there are many, if any, persons who had such a deep involvement in these issues over such an extended and critical period in the history of Texas redistricting. Thus, as readers go through the following chapters, they will have the benefit of the perspective of an author who was, in the words of the musical *Hamilton*, literally in the room where it happened.

From 1974 to 1976, Steve served as parliamentarian of the Texas Senate. While that span did not include a decennial redistricting session, it gave Steve the opportunity to gain a real insight into the legislative process and an understanding and appreciation of the members and leaders of the legislature—knowledge that would be invaluable in subsequent years as he advised legislators during the redistricting process and defended their actions in the courts.

Following his service as senate parliamentarian, Steve became an assistant attorney general under Attorney General John Hill. As a special assistant and later as the chief of the State and County Affairs Division of the Office of the Attorney General, Steve assumed responsibilities in defending the state in the ongoing lawsuits that lingered following the redistricting that reflected the results of the 1970 census. This included the landmark case of *Graves v. Barnes* (later *White v. Regester*) discussed in this book.

When John Hill's tenure as attorney general ended in 1978, Steve moved to San Antonio to work with the legendary Herb Kelleher, one of the founders of Southwest Airlines, who at the time was general counsel of the airline company and a partner in his own law firm. Steve worked on the legal issues associated with Southwest's transformation from an intrastate to an interstate airline. During that time, he also had a contract with the Texas Senate to prepare a legal and historical guide to redistricting for the use of the Texas Senate in the coming 1981 legislative session, when the legislature would redistrict following the publication of the 1980 census.

Steve decided to leave the San Antonio practice and invited me to join him in starting our own two-person law firm, Bickerstaff, Heath LLP; the contract with the senate was one of our first pieces of legal work. The analysis he produced pursuant to that contract was subsequently published in book form by the Texas Legislative Council, an abridged version of which can be found as "Reapportionment by State Legislatures: A Guide for the 1980s," *SMU Law Review 34:2* (1980). More important, it became a resource for both the House and senate as they undertook the task of drawing legislative districts that, due to the 1975 extension to Texas of Section 5 of the Voting Rights Act (VRA), would be required for the first time to be submitted to the Department of Justice for preclearance before those newly adopted districts could be used in an election. As discussed in more detail in chapter 6, the complexities in that process ran the gamut of issues that can come up in legislative redistricting.

While the guide Steve wrote for the Texas Senate largely set the template for the redistricting effort, lawmakers did not always follow his recommendations. In particular, the Texas House of Representatives decided not to follow his advice on avoiding cutting county boundaries in favor of conflicting, but more politically palatable, advice from some lawyer-legislators. As a result, the House districts were found to violate the state constitution. During that redistricting session, the two houses of the legislature were controlled by Democrats, but the governor, Bill Clements, was a Republican.

Because the way district lines are drawn can have a decided partisan effect, any instance in which a state is under divided political control makes it difficult to yield a final redistricting product. In this case, the Republican governor vetoed the redistricting plan adopted by the Democrat-controlled senate. Since the House plan had been invalidated by the Texas Supreme Court because of its failure to respect county boundaries and the senate plan had been vetoed, the task of drawing legislative districts passed to the Legislative Redistricting Board (LRB)—a body established by the state constitution to assume the redistricting task if the legislature failed to successfully adopt a plan.

The LRB consists of the lieutenant governor, the Speaker of the House, the attorney general, the comptroller of public accounts, and the commissioner of the General Land Office. Steve then had the opportunity to advise the LRB and later to defend the legislative and congressional plans when they were challenged in court. This included his work in *Upham v. Seamon*, a landmark case that defined the relationship between the courts and the legislature when it comes to adopting maps.

Steve was not directly involved in the legislative redistricting following the 1990 census, but in 2001 he advised Attorney General John Cornyn in his role as chair of the Legislative Redistricting Board. The year 2001 was a pivotal one in Texas redistricting history. Republicans, whose party by that time was dominant, could see a path to cementing their position through redistricting. In particular, the process provided the opportunity for them to achieve a majority in the House of Representatives, which, due to the district lines drawn by Democrats following the 1990 census, retained a Democratic majority.

The 2001 legislature, charged with drawing the new House, senate, and congressional districts, consisted of a senate with a Republican majority and a Democrat-majority House of Representatives. The governor, as well as all statewide elected officials—including the four statewide elected officials on the LRB—were Republican. Because the legislature was under divided control, with Democrats in charge of one chamber and Republicans in control of the other, any redistricting plans that could be adopted would likely reflect a compromise between the parties. If, however, as ultimately happened, the Republicans could prevent the legislature from passing any plan, the redistricting task would pass to the LRB, most of whose members were Republican. The LRB approved House and senate plans that increased the number of Republican seats and, for the first time, produced a Republican majority in the House of Representatives.

The LRB has no jurisdiction over congressional districts, so those districts were drawn by a federal court. The court was required, pursuant to *Upham v. Seamon*, to give deference to the latest expression of legislative will regarding congressional districts. This was the plan adopted following the 1990 census by a legislature in which Democrats were in control and that produced a districting plan that favored Democrats. As a result, the 2001 court-ordered plan that was generally based on that earlier plan produced a congressional delegation with a 17–15 Democratic majority.

When the 2003 legislature, which now had both a House and senate with Republican majorities, convened, it proceeded to replace the court-ordered plan with a new one drawn by the legislature. This was sometimes known as the re-re-districting. After the districts were redrawn, the court-ordered plan that had a 17–15 Democratic majority ended up as a legislatively drawn plan that, by the end of the decade, produced a 23–9 Republican majority. This was the legislative session in which Republican voting strength was converted to control all elements of statewide political power in Texas. The House of Representatives, the senate, and the congressional delegation all had Republican majorities.

All statewide elected officials were Republicans. The state in which in the 1960s a single elected Republican was a rarity was now clearly a Republican stronghold. Although Steve did not participate in the 2003 congressional redistricting, he was thoroughly familiar with it and wrote a book—*Lines in the Sand: Congressional Redistricting in Texas and the Downfall of Tom Delay* (University of Texas Press, 2007)—about it. This was the redistricting session in which House Democrats fled to Ardmore, Oklahoma, and subsequently senate Democrats traveled to Albuquerque, New Mexico, in what proved to be unsuccessful attempts to prevent the congressional redistricting bill's passage.

While these last few paragraphs have discussed Steve's ties to redistricting at the state level, which is the subject of this book, he also was intimately involved in representing cities, counties, and school districts when they redrew their single-member districts. Essentially, the same legal principles apply whether the redistricting is of state or local government.

In each decade of his professional tenure, Steve and the law firm represented numerous political subdivisions as they drew districts following the census or otherwise faced legal questions in a redistricting context. In recent years, the firm has represented roughly a hundred local jurisdictions during a redistricting cycle. Steve and the firm would also represent local governments in redistricting-related litigation.

In 1998, Steve retired from the law firm to pursue business opportunities and to teach at the University of Texas School of Law, where his classes and seminars addressed election law and redistricting. Although he retired as a partner in the law firm, he continued to do occasional legal work, including work on the 2001 redistricting. During that period of his career, he was a Fulbright Scholar teaching in Germany and a Rockefeller Foundation Scholar in Italy. In addition to this posthumously published book, he authored *Election Systems and Gerrymandering Worldwide*, which was published in Europe shortly after his death.

Steve was an excellent lawyer. He was always thoroughly prepared and, like a chess master who can visualize the board many moves ahead, he brought insight and prescience to his analysis of legal issues. It is likely that there is no one who had as intimate, as long, and as knowledgeable a relationship with Texas redistricting as Steve Bickerstaff. For the reader who wants to learn about this important aspect of the state's legal and political history, this book is the place to start.

C. ROBERT HEATH, DECEMBER 2019

ACKNOWLEDGMENTS

BOB HEATH REVIEWED AND HELPED edit this book. His assistance was invaluable. Bob is recognized nationwide as one of the ablest and most experienced redistricting attorneys. He has previously served as assistant to a Texas state senator, as clerk for US District Judge Jack Roberts, and as Chief of the Opinions Division of the Office of the Texas Attorney General. Bob co-founded the private law firm of Bickerstaff, Heath LLP in 1980. Over the past thirty-nine years, he has represented dozens of public jurisdictions and officials in election and open-government matters and is the author of several consequential articles on these legal issues. He is now a senior partner at Bickerstaff Heath Delgado Acosta LLP.

I also wish to acknowledge Charlotte Carter, whose patience and copyediting skills made this book possible.

STEVE BICKERSTAFF, AUGUST 2019

INTRODUCTION

JIM DUNNAM WAS IN THE parking lot of the Embassy Suites in Austin on Sunday afternoon, May 11, 2003. He was alone in his thoughts as he anxiously awaited his colleagues, the Democrats of the Texas House of Representatives. As chairman of the House Democratic Caucus, he knew that he was on the verge of either a historic walkout that would defeat the Republicans' congressional redistricting legislation or a shameful fiasco. The planned walkout was the Democrats' last and least-favored option.

To break a quorum in the Texas House of Representatives so that it cannot pass legislation requires the absence of fifty-one members, one more than one third of the 150 members. The margin for error was narrow. There were sixty-two Democrats in the House, but the price to be paid for participating in the walkout would be steep. The Republican Speaker of the House, Tom Craddick, was certain to exact revenge. As a result, getting over fifty-one Democrats to secretly sign a pledge to leave had been difficult.

As he waited in the parking lot, Dunnam went over the numbers in his head. He knew that Democratic Representative Ron Wilson had come out openly for the Republican legislation and that for various reasons eight Democrats would remain in Austin where they were likely, willingly or unwillingly, to become part of the House quorum. Six other Democrats pledged to join the boycott by traveling out of state on their own. If all kept their promises, the House would be without a quorum. If not . . . ?

The Democrats came to the parking lot slowly. They arrived alone or in small groups. Dunnam was anxious. Some Democrats were driving around and watching or receiving cell phone reports on the number of arrivals. They wanted to make sure the walkout would be successful before they joined it. Those already in the buses called their absent colleagues to encourage them to come. Dunnam waited and worried.

Meanwhile, the Speaker, Republican Tom Craddick, was in his apartment at the back of the House chamber, totally unaware of the Democrats' plans. He was furious when he learned that the Democrats were gone. Their absence jeopardized the Republican plan to gain control of the Texas congressional delegation for the first time since shortly after the Civil War. Craddick immediately called the other state officials (all Republicans), Congressman Tom DeLay, and the Department of Public Safety (DPS). The message was similar in each call: "Find the Democrats and bring them to the House chamber." To the public he said, "The Chicken Ds that did this ought to be ashamed of themselves. There is disgrace in running and hiding. . . . I've been in the House for thirty-five years and I've lost some, but I've never walked off the floor like these Chicken Ds."

The Democrats' walkout captured the nation's, and to some extent the world's, attention for months in 2003. The question is: Why such drastic tactics for this particular moment?

The tactic of House Democrats—and subsequently senate Democrats—to flee the state en masse to deny a quorum and prevent action on a congressional redistricting bill was extreme. Extreme action, however, was not entirely unexpected in 2003. That year marked a tectonic shift in the balance of partisan power in Texas. Historically, Texas, like other states in the south, had been a Democratic state. When the modern era of redistricting pursuant to the one-person, one-vote principle began in 1965, only one Republican served in the 150-member Texas House of Representatives. There were no Republicans among the thirty-one state senators. Over the years, however, the Texas Republican Party gained strength with each succeeding election. Democrats had seen their majority in the state senate evaporate by the end of the 1990s and their majority in the House of Representatives dismantled by the 2001 LRB redistricting. By 2003, there was a Republican governor and Republican majorities in both the Texas House of Representatives and the state senate.

Two years earlier, a federal court had drawn congressional districts for the state because the legislature could not agree on a districting plan. In 2001, Democrats still had a majority in the House of Representatives, and Republicans had a majority in the state senate. If the move to replace the court-drawn congressional redistricting plan with one drawn by the new legislature (where Republicans were now in complete control) came to a vote, Democrats would not be able to prevent the codification of a very unfavorable map for them. For Democrats, 2003 marked desperate times calling for desperate measures.

The legislature considers many important issues, yet redistricting—the redrawing of district lines generally following the once-a-decade census to bring districts into population balance—is one of very few that invariably seizes the interest of legislators and the public and that can result in extraordinary measures such as a third of the legislative body fleeing the state for an extended period to prevent action on that or any other legislation. Why is that?

Redistricting has an impact on at least three distinct groups. First, it affects the individual legislators, since it determines the composition of the districts in which they must seek reelection. Second, it affects political parties and may determine whether a particular party will be able to control a majority of legislative seats and thereby shape public policy in the state for the coming decade. Finally, it affects racial and ethnic groups and may determine if candidates from those groups will have an opportunity to be elected. In essence, redistricting can, and often does, determine who will be elected in a given district.

The annals of redistricting are replete with situations where districts are designed to ensure a legislator's reelection or promotion to a higher office such as a congressional seat. In 1971, the 18th Congressional District was drawn with the expectation that State Senator Barbara Jordan would run in it and win, which she did. In other instances, districts are drawn to separate an incumbent from his base of support. Chapter 4 explains how a Democratic legislature drew West Texas districts to prevent Republican Congressman Ed Foreman from being reelected, and chapter 7 discusses how a Republican legislature drew districts in Dallas and East Texas to successfully prevent the reelection of Democratic incumbents Martin Frost and Jim Turner. Any politician's continued electoral viability is of the utmost importance to that individual. It follows then that a senator or representative may often consider redistricting legislation to be the single most important item on the legislative agenda.

In addition to the impact redistricting has on individual members of the legislature and of Congress, it can also determine which political party will be successful and which may be relegated to minority status for the next decade. A skillfully drawn redistricting plan can ensure that a political party retains a majority of a state's legislative or congressional seats even though it does not receive a majority of the votes. For example, in Pennsylvania, in the three elections of the 2012 to 2016 cycle, Democrats received, on average, 51 percent of the vote to the Republicans' 49 percent. Yet, due to the 2011 redistricting plan drawn by the Republican-controlled General Assembly, Republicans consistently elected their candidates to thirteen congressional seats while the Democrats were successful in only five. The Pennsylvania Republicans drew districts that benefited their candidates; in

Texas, much the same result was evident, but for another party in a previous era. Because of the manner in which districts were drawn in the early 1990s, when the Democrats were in control, Democrats were able to maintain a state House of Representatives and a congressional delegation majority until the turn of the century, even though Republicans garnered more votes.

Redistricting also has a major impact on racial and ethnic minorities. Racially polarized voting is a fact of life in many areas. This simply means that people are more likely to vote for candidates of their race or ethnic group and, conversely, against candidates of other racial or ethnic groups. Thus, if districts are drawn so that a geographically compact group— of, for example, African Americans—is split among multiple districts so that the group is in a minority in each district, it will be difficult for candidates of that race to be elected. On the other hand, if the group is not split but instead is placed in a single district, then it likely will have a good chance in that district of electing candidates favored by African Americans.

Under the Voting Rights Act and court decisions made under that act and the Fourteenth and Fifteenth Amendments, districts must be drawn to avoid discriminating against racial and ethnic groups. As a result, legislative bodies, which were once almost always all white, now are much more racially and ethnically diverse. During the redistricting process, legislators will look to their individual and partisan interests, but they must do so in the context of complying with legal requirements. Generally, this means making sure that the districts are in population balance and that they do not discriminate against racial or ethnic minorities.

The effort to draw districts that conform to the nondiscriminatory requirements of the Voting Rights Act will raise the most difficult and salient legal issues during a legislature's consideration of redistricting bills. This is an issue important both to Texas and nationwide. Indeed, the demography of Texas may predict demographic changes in the rest of the United States. A 2019 article in *The New York Times* asked, "Is San Antonio Our Political Future?" The article's point was that San Antonio is a "majority minority" city with 64 percent of its residents Hispanic. For that matter, a majority of Texas residents are now Hispanic, African American, or Asian, the latter constituting the fastest growing category. Hispanics are likely to become the largest category of ethnic-minority Texans by 2022 but are unlikely to be a majority until the latter part of the twenty-first century. The population of the United States is rapidly becoming more diverse and one day soon may become majority minority. Texas provides a model for this change, and the way Texas addresses this demographic evolution may offer lessons—for good or ill—for the rest of the country.

Because the districts drawn every redistricting cycle determine whom we will elect to write our laws and to guide our state and nation, the decisions made during the redistricting process have an immense effect on how we are governed. They will affect whether our policy fairly reflects the will of the people, including all parts of our diverse citizenry, or whether the will of the majority is thwarted because skillful line drawing made possible the repeated election of members who do not reflect the majority view. Understanding the redistricting process is important for both legislators and citizens, as redistricting in a fair and responsible manner is critical to our representative democracy.

The effects of a single redistricting can reach far beyond the outcome of the subsequent election. The district boundaries drawn at the beginning of a decade affect outcomes for the next ten years, or longer. For example, in 1981 the contiguous South Texas counties of Cameron and Hidalgo could have been joined to form a single compact congressional district that had the ideal population. The incumbent Hispanic congressman favored this configuration and Hispanic activist organizations testified before the Texas Legislature on its behalf. I was an attorney advising the State and thought the conjoined district was noncontroversial given the circumstances. However, a Hispanic activist organization that had earlier written and testified in favor of the compact configuration changed its position and after the session challenged the district configuration in federal court under the Voting Rights Act on the basis that Hispanic voting strength could be enhanced if the two heavily Hispanic counties were split to form the foundation for two majority Hispanic districts. The federal court agreed. The single compact district gave way to two elongated districts that stretched from the Rio Grande to near San Antonio. These districts have been maintained with minimal change for the past forty years and are a testament to how the effects of a single redistricting may linger far into the future. Once a district is drawn, there is pressure from the incumbent and others to retain that configuration going forward.

The process of redistricting is also the story of Texas, how it has been drawn and how it has been politically constituted. Redistricting renders the story of Texans as they are counted and represented. The story I relate here also shows how the dominance of the Democrats for the initial century and a quarter of Texas history foreshadowed precisely how the Republicans would grab and maintain power over the course of my career. Gerrymandering has been at the heart of many famous moments in Texas history and provides a roadmap to our likely political future in the Lone Star State. There are times when the history depicted here reads somewhat differently from the accustomed story of the glory of Texas and the heroism of Texans. It is no less true.

I was born in Texas and have been a resident of this state all my life. I am proud to be a Texan, but that does not mean that I am proud of everything that has been done in the name of the State of Texas. Gerrymandering has corroded our democracy and strangled public faith in our civic institutions. After studying this problem my entire life, litigating it for forty years, researching and writing about it, and, above all, watching it happen, I propose a few solutions that would undo some of the damage wrought by partisan redistricting.

The Texas tale of lawmaking in general, and redistricting specifically, is often filled with contention, self-interest, and grasps for power. I have tried to depict this story accurately, with both its beauty marks and its blemishes.

GERRY MAND ERING

TEXAS

CHAPTER 1

REDISTRICTING AND GERRYMANDERING

THE POPULATION AND DEMOGRAPHICS of the United States are always changing. In addition to the cycles of birth and death, cities and states grow and shrink alongside the boom and bust of a given local economy. Think of all the people who left their hometowns for education and employment and then never returned. Consider the 86,200 people who moved from California to Texas in 2018. All these population shifts must be accounted for in our representative democracy. These people must be apportioned into districts that will, in part, define the election chances of the people who decide to run for office there. Redistricting is the way we take account of this change and keep the democratic process current.

Although each legislative redrawing of congressional and state legislative districts in Texas over the past 184 years involved some unique elements, there are many significant issues that furnish threads throughout the period. These general tools and tactics have been modified and bastardized by various political actors across Texas history but, broadly speaking, this chapter details how the process gets done.

First, some definitions. The words "apportionment" and "districting" often are used interchangeably by both scholars and the courts. This interchangeable usage sometimes creates confusion. In a technical sense, the words are not synonymous. To apportion seats in a legislative body is to allocate those seats among usually predefined geographical areas or political jurisdictions. On the other hand, districting (or redistricting) is the actual drawing of the geographical boundaries of the electoral areas from which the members of the legislative body are elected. For other democracies and many political scientists, the word "delimitation" (i.e., to set out limits or boundaries) is often used instead of apportionment or districting. So, for example, it is common to refer to the redistricting of the areas from which members of local-government governing boards are elected even though the geographical areas in question, such as precincts or wards, are sometimes not actually called districts.

The best example of apportionment (or reapportionment) is, of course, the allocation of seats in Congress among the fifty states after each decennial census. The US Census is conducted on April 1 of the last year of a decade and is required by the US Constitution to be a count of every inhabitant of every place in the nation, however remote, on that date. The current census not only counts persons but also surveys a wide variety of information about conditions and people. This information is collected, organized, and released in a series of reports, now largely contained in electronic form, over several years.

The first release of census data in the US comes early in the year following that in which the census is conducted and relates population data, including race and voting age, for all geographic areas in the country. The measured data yields information down to small areas generally equivalent to a city block. This detail, combined with computer software designed specifically for redistricting, generally shows that the electoral districts are unequal in population and allows state legislatures, local government officials, redistricting commissions, and the general public to draw and proffer redistricting plans based on the new population data.

Each state is entitled to at least one seat in the US House of Representatives. Congress apportions the remaining 385 seats based on the relative number of persons in each state but does not draw the actual districts. As a result of the 2010 census, for instance, Texas was apportioned four new seats in Congress. The other states gaining seats were Florida (which gained two representatives), Arizona, Georgia, Nevada, South Carolina, Utah, and Washington (which each gained one representative). These twelve reapportioned seats came from New York and Ohio (which each lost two representatives), Illinois, Iowa, Louisiana, Massachusetts, Michigan, Missouri, New Jersey, and Pennsylvania (which each lost one representative). In those seven states entitled to only one representative in 2011 (Alaska, Delaware, Montana, North Dakota, South Dakota, Vermont, and Wyoming), the entire state is the district. In the other states, the state legislature or other entity designated by state law draws the boundaries of the congressional districts.

In Texas, the congressional as well as the state legislative districts are drawn by the state legislature based on this census data. This occurs unless, as I describe later in this book, the state or federal courts or the Legislative Redistricting Board are required to draw the districts because the legislature has failed to act or has adopted unlawful plans. For state legislative seats, however, the formula is less clear. In Texas, the earliest constitutions envisioned a process for the Texas House of Representatives similar in some respects to the one in Congress, with the allocation of legislative seats among the state's counties. Initially, each county was guaranteed at least one member of this lower chamber of the Texas Legislature. The legislature determined the actual number of representatives per county, who were then elected county-wide (i.e., at-large).

By 1875, the year of the writing of the current Texas Constitution, it was impossible to guarantee a seat for each county because the number of counties exceeded the number of representatives allowed by the Constitution. The Constitution, however, still required that the seats be apportioned among the counties but assigned the legislature to draw the districts by combining counties or parts of counties when necessary to form representative districts. Even today, when districts are primarily drawn to equalize population, there remains an element of apportionment in the allocation of Texas House seats among counties in accordance with the constitutional formula.

I use the words "apportionment" and "districting" interchangeably in this book. Except in the circumstance of action by Congress, my choice of wording generally denotes only a personal preference in a specific context and not a substantive difference.

REDISTRICTING LEGISLATION

Electoral districts are established by the Texas Legislature through bills that become law only if they pass both chambers of the legislature and the governor signs them or allows them to become law. There are, however, several aspects of that process that should be noted.

The Texas Legislature has routinely considered separate bills for state senate, state House of Representatives, and congressional districts. A senate bill enacts senate districts. A House bill enacts House districts. The bill establishing congressional districts can originate in either chamber. There is usually only a single bill for each category of districts, which is drawn up in the respective redistricting committee of each chamber after public hearing.

Each chamber must pass the other chamber's bill for it to be enacted. Like other legislation, bills originating in either chamber are theoretically subject to amendment by the other chamber. The tradition in Texas has been for each chamber generally to pass the other's redistricting legislation without debate or change, so each chamber in effect does its own redistricting. On the other hand, the bill enacting the congressional districts is often controversial within and between the chambers and may see many changes. This difference in part explains why it has become traditional for congressional redistricting to be done after the regular legislative session in a special session called to consider the specific topic. Sometimes, as in 1981, 1992, and 2003, the governor's authority to call special sessions has been weaponized in the political fight between the two dominant parties.

Initially, redistricting legislation assigned whole counties within each electoral district. As the number of persons and counties grew, it became necessary to partition some counties to achieve voter equality. Some of these splits were defined in the terms of real estate at the time, as in metes and bounds. Now, it is possible to describe electoral districts using a mixture of whole counties and census geography, such as census block or election precinct Voting Tabulation Districts (VTDs) data.

Redistricting legislation is ordinarily subject to the same rules as are applicable to other legislation. For example, it was possible for the Democrats in the Texas House to kill the congressional redistricting legislation during the 2003 regular session by preventing action on the bill until so late in the session that House rules prohibited consideration of any House bill. On the other hand, special rules may be adopted. For instance, in 1981, the Texas Senate considered senate and congressional redistricting in a "Committee of the Whole Senate" to allow each senator to hear testimony that would typically be heard only by members of the Senate Redistricting Committee.

Redistricting legislation can be vetoed by the governor. In 1981, Republican governor Bill Clements vetoed the bill establishing the new senate districts, sending the issue to the Legislative Redistricting Board. He also vetoed the legislature's congressional redistricting plan, setting off a contest of wills that lasted through three special sessions. On several occasions, elections were held under plans approved by the LRB or federal courts after the Texas Legislature either failed to act or enacted invalid plans. Many of these stories are taken up in later chapters.

THE TEXAS LEGISLATIVE REDISTRICTING BOARD

Under Article III, Section 28, of the Texas Constitution, a Legislative Redistricting Board is tasked with reapportioning the state's legislative districts, but not congressional or State Board of Education districts, if the legislature fails to do so in its first regular session after publication of the federal decennial census. As previously noted, the LRB consists of five elected officials: the lieutenant governor, the attorney general, the comptroller of public accounts, the commissioner of the General Land Office, and the Speaker of the House of Representatives. The only LRB member not elected statewide is the Speaker, who is elected by the 150 members of the lower chamber of the legislature. Noticeable in absence from this board is the governor. Unlike a legislative enactment, an apportionment plan adopted by the LRB is not subject to gubernatorial veto.

The LRB was created by constitutional amendment adopted by the legislature in 1947 and passed by the voters in 1948. It was considered a means by which legislators could be forced to redistrict in the first legislative session after release of the decennial census or face the prospect that the LRB would do it for them. However, the constitutional provision does not give the LRB authority to redraw congressional districts. Therefore, it has become routine for the legislature to leave congressional redistricting to be done in a special legislative session after adjournment of the regular session.

For three of the past five decades, the LRB has been called on to redistrict the Texas Senate or House of Representatives. Each time, many of the same disputes that affected the legislature resurfaced at the LRB. Even when all or a majority of the LRB were from the same political party, the members of the board often disagreed mightily about which redistricting plan to adopt.

THE TOOLS OF REDISTRICTING

The basic tools of redistricting are relatively simple. Most come directly from the US decennial census. They include accurate maps of the area to be redistricted and the existing districts; counts of persons in an area (this data should be available for the smallest geographical areas possible); and means of calculating the data. The object is to describe the electoral districts so that they meet certain public-interest criteria, such as equality in population, contiguity, compactness, preservation of communities of interest, and recognition of natural features (e.g., rivers, lakes, mountains, etc. that could influence travel within a district). Many states explicitly provide these criteria in their constitutions or laws. The Texas Constitution establishes only a few such criteria. Article III, Section 25, provides: "The State shall be divided into Senatorial Districts of contiguous territory, and each district shall be entitled to elect one Senator." Section 26 of Article III provides: "The members of the House of Representatives shall be apportioned among the several counties, according to the number of population in each," with a few exceptions. There are no criteria mandated for congressional districts.

In one sense, little about redistricting has changed over the last 180 years. The same problems of personal and political self-interest persist. On the other hand, technology has made redistricting and gerrymandering easier.

In the 1970s, we would spread large census maps (often several at a time) on the floor and use a calculator to add or subtract figures in the Census Bureau's population booklets to determine a district's population. Computers were first used for this purpose in the '80s, but it took at least a day to "run" each plan and errors were sometimes committed. On one occasion, a computer technician discovered after a plan had been adopted that it had inadvertently left out several miscellaneous census blocks in Williamson County. It was my task to explain to the members of the Legislative Redistricting Board how such an error could occur and to ask that an order be adopted *nunc pro tunc* to correct the mistake. Now, software developed specially for redistricting allows a person to manipulate census and political data on a laptop and know in seconds the effect of moving a single election precinct. The architects of the 2003 redrawing of the congressional district plan told me that it was like a computer game, with the contestants trying to devise the most partisan plan possible.

Technology improves each decade and plays a major role in redistricting. Computers with GIS (geographic information system) software can calculate data and display proffered redistricting plans in seconds that only three decades ago took hours of work and reams of paper to construct. Specific software for redistricting is being used at every level of government in the United States. This technology makes redistricting easier, faster, and more accurate for those charged with the task, but it also has the same benefits for people wanting to gerrymander districts.

GERRYMANDERING

Since the word itself has crept into the explanation of the redistricting process, here is an opportune point at which to define gerrymandering. Gerrymandering is the design of the boundaries of electoral districts so that an incumbent or a dominant political party has an election advantage. In some instances, it has meant the failure to redistrict at all. Changing districts to accommodate democratic changes may be divisive, even among members of the same political party. With this political infighting, one may understand why maintaining the status quo is often the easiest option. For many decades, Texas, like many other states, was gripped by legislative gridlock over redistricting because any change in district boundaries was contrary to the self-interest of those making the decision.

Essentially, a gerrymander occurs when self-interest is substituted for the public's interest. Texas has not avoided this practice. Both major parties have engaged in it. Sometimes it has achieved its purpose, and sometimes not.

In recent years, there has been an outcry in the United States against gerrymandering electoral districts. Opponents of the practice charge that voters should choose their politicians rather than allowing politicians to choose their voters. This aphorism is a general truth but is an oversimplification of the complex processes and competing interests that affect the redrawing of election districts. Gerrymandering is about power, control, and political survival and has been reconstituted across our history for the needs of each particular moment.

Gerrymandering ordinarily begins with the avoidance of putting two or more incumbents in the same electoral district—that is, "pairing" the incumbents. However, sometimes this practice is impossible because of significant demographic changes in the districts. For example, as rural counties in

Texas have grown slowly, or not at all, it has become necessary in the past to combine all or parts of existing districts in
which these rural counties were located. This situation often
led to pairing two or more incumbents. It is usually hoped
that at least one of the incumbents is retiring so that actual
election contests can be avoided.

This avoidance of pairing is often done on behalf of the
incumbents of both parties. There are many reasons why
incumbents do not wish to be paired. On occasion, pairing—or the threat of pairing—in Texas has been used as
an offensive weapon. For example, conservative Democrat
Gus Mutscher was accused in 1971 of using his power as
Speaker of the state House of Representatives to pair liberal
Democrats and Republicans in the same district to rid the
House of some of his enemies. The most notorious use of pairing as an offensive weapon came in 2003, when many incumbent Democratic congressmen were paired with incumbent
Republican congressmen in districts specifically drawn to
favor the Republican. On the other extreme are those electoral districts that have grown substantially in population
over the prior decade and must "shed" persons to avoid being
overpopulated in the new redistricting plan. Most representatives are reluctant to "lose" any part of a district in which
they won election but, if legally forced to do so, they want to
be sure to select the right area and persons to lose.

An additional bit of information is needed for gerrymandering that does not apply to basic redistricting. Gerrymandering
generally works only if the housing pattern in an area is politically segregated so that most persons living in an identified
geographical area dependably vote for the same candidates or
political party. A politically homogeneous area is less susceptible to gerrymandering. Reliable information about how persons have voted in the past can be used to predict how they will
likely vote in the future. Some jurisdictions nationwide have
prohibited the use of such political data.

Information on how individuals vote is not directly available in the census data. However, in preparation for the 1980 census, the Census Bureau began experimenting with the possibility of reporting data by Voting Tabulation Districts, which generally corresponded to election precincts. These VTDs were created to make it easier to equalize population among districts, but it was simple for the Texas Legislative Council to match the election data from each election precinct in the state to a corresponding VTD. This feat could be achieved only for recent elections because the boundaries of the election precincts were constantly being changed by the Texas counties, but for the first time Texas had an official tool to allow areas to be grouped together or split apart based on how voters in the areas had voted in the past. This conversion of census data to precincts and election data to VTDs remains an area susceptible to possible mistakes, but gerrymandering became easier.

Election patterns, however, are often volatile. It is crucial then to select the right elections to serve as benchmarks for determining an area's voting tendency. For example, in 2018, would the vote in the Ted Cruz vs. Beto O'Rourke race for US senator or that of the Greg Abbott vs. Lupe Valdez race for governor provide a more reliable indicator of partisan support in an area? By using several elections to give a range of results, it is possible to ascertain the highs and lows of past support in an area for specific candidates or parties. Choosing the right past elections for comparison is key. Again, computers can dependably analyze complex statistics and prior election results.

Often, however, the designation of "friendly" and "unfriendly" areas for purposes of gerrymandering results not from any detailed or technical analysis but from a politician's practical experience or sentiment, such as an incumbent's feeling that "they love me there." The adoption of a gerrymander is far more dependent on politics than technology—or, as famously voiced regarding constituencies in the United Kingdom, "a constituency is created, not found."

This original (now infamous) 1812 gerrymander cartoon depicts the Essex South state senatorial district for the legislature of The Commonwealth of Massachusetts.

The custom of designing electoral districts for political advantage dates to the earliest use of districts for elections. This practice was given a name ("Gerry-mander") in the *Boston Gazette* on March 26, 1812, when the word was first used to describe a redrawing of Massachusetts State Senate election districts by the Massachusetts Legislature during the term of Governor Elbridge Gerry. One of the districts was claimed to resemble the shape of a mythological salamander. The word "gerrymander" is a combination of the governor's last name and the word salamander.

The 1812 "Gerry-mander" was drawn to benefit Governor Gerry's Democratic-Republican Party. The precise purpose presents an enigma. If the district were drawn so that Gerry's party could win it, the gerrymander failed. The opposing Federalist Party candidate won this district by over 15 percent. However, if the district were created to pack Federalist voters and drain them from the other senatorial districts, it was a success. The overall redistricting successfully resulted in the reelection of a Democratic-Republican majority in the Massachusetts State Senate.

The first legislative gerrymanders in Texas occurred when counties were grouped by the Republic's Congress to form senate districts and to determine which counties merited more than one representative. These decisions were primarily driven by whom the Congress had decided should be counted (e.g., not slaves nor their descendants). Similar gerrymandering persisted once Texas became a state of the US.

TYPES OF GERRYMANDERING

Gerrymandering occurs for several reasons but can generally be boiled down to two: partisan advantage and incumbent protection.

The theory behind the partisan gerrymander is to draw electoral district boundaries in a plan such that, taken as a whole, the plan gives the dominant party or group the best chance of winning enough seats to continue to control the legislative process and to help party incumbents win reelection without harming the party's overall objectives. This goal is achieved through the shaping of electoral districts in such a way that the probable votes for an opposing candidate or party are wasted. A political party wants to achieve a result that satisfies its members and guarantees the best chance for electing its candidates. A gerrymander for an incumbent usually means maintaining the status quo as nearly as possible by creating electoral district boundaries shaped for the benefit of incumbents seeking reelection.

A single-member district will usually resemble or remain unchanged from the boundary of the district in which the incumbent was elected in the past. The boundary may be changed to make the incumbent's reelection more likely by the removal of areas in which most of the voters were expected to oppose the incumbent's reelection or the addition of areas in which the voters are expected to support the incumbent. Each incumbent is usually eager to find "friendly" voters to help his or her reelection, but often incumbents from the same party have their eyes on the same areas or voters. The intra-party fight over these voters can become desperate, especially if the incumbents believe that their reelection depends on the outcome of the dispute.

Not all members of the Texas Legislature start out with an intention to gerrymander the electoral district in which they were elected, or any other district. The idea of gerrymandering may be abhorrent to them. Nevertheless, as the redistricting process proceeds, these members often find that if they remain passive, they soon become victims. Some other members may have fewer scruples about gerrymandering or may have become desperate about their chances for reelection unless they find more friendly voters, a place to which they can jettison some unfriendly ones, or have an underpopulated district. Any change to satisfy one member affects other districts, and the changes thereafter ripple through any proffered plan.

A passive member can find that his or her current district has been deprived of its friendly voters or has become the dumping ground for unfriendly ones to help another member. The passive member's abhorrence of gerrymandering becomes a regrettable fight for survival. I have often seen members who initially profess that they "do not care" about the makeup of their districts but subsequently become aggressive defenders of their current district's boundaries.

The one most certainly illegal gerrymander has to do with racial or ethnic discrimination. Such a gerrymander is unlawful in the US under the Constitution and Section 2 of the Voting Rights Act, if the minority group is large enough, politically cohesive, and has historically seen its candidates lose because of the voting of a polarized majority.

Some gerrymanders are incidental. A gerrymander may not be the result of a Machiavellian conspiracy to affect an election outcome. I have seen candidates gerrymander a district's boundary to exclude a possible opponent's residence, to include the residence of a family member or influential person, to include a prestigious institution such as a university or medical facility, or to include or exclude areas for seemingly trivial or undisclosed reasons. However, virtually all such mundane requests have the ultimate objective of creating some political benefit for the incumbent, such as an opportunity for less competition, a less expensive campaign, greater prestige, or larger campaign contributions.

These reasons overlap. For example, a political party that is in power is likely to want to protect its incumbents and therefore is interested in preventing any changes that could adversely affect them. The options for gerrymandering must face the political realities of the legislative body, however. Sometimes the result desired by the dominant party cannot be achieved. For incumbents, sometimes it can be achieved only with the cooperation of other incumbents, even members of an opposing party. It is common in such circumstances for the incumbents from two or more parties to negotiate an agreed course of action that protects the incumbents of both parties. Further, a gerrymander that advantages a party or incumbent may have the effect of disadvantaging a racial or ethnic minority. While one result (partisan gerrymandering) is legal and the other (racial gerrymandering) is not, the true purpose of the gerrymander may be obscure.

THE TACTICS OF GERRYMANDERING

The five classic tactics of gerrymandering single-member districts are known as "cracking," "packing," maintaining the status quo, population inequality, and the use of at-large or multi-member districts to submerge political minorities. All have existed in Texas.

Cracking occurs when voters that historically vote dependably for opposition candidates or political parties are intentionally split among two or more districts in such a way that these voters are submerged in a majority that is likely to vote for a competing candidate or political party. Opposition votes are essentially wasted because the candidates supported by a majority of pro-government voters always win.

Cracking the opposition means, however, that the voters intended to be in the majority are also spread among the districts to create as many districts as needed in which the candidates or party favored by the government will win. It also requires reliable information about how persons have voted in the past and judgment about how they will likely vote in the future. If the friendly voters are spread too thin, an unexpected voting pattern that benefits the opposing candidates may cause the favored candidates to lose in some districts where they anticipated winning. Thus, it behooves the gerrymander drawer to search for the right balance, systematically spreading the voters among the districts so that the candidates or party favored by the government will win in as many districts as needed to control the legislature without unnecessarily creating the possibility of losing if the voting pattern changes. The objective from a party's perspective is the total plan, not necessarily winning a single district.

A second method of wasting votes for opposing candidates or political parties is known as packing. As the name suggests, this method is aimed at placing as many of the opposing candidate's or party's voters in as few districts as possible.

A pro-government candidate will have little or no chance of winning in these districts because the voters are overwhelmingly likely to vote for the opposition, but the effect of packing the opposition's voters in only a few districts is to allow the pro-government candidates to more easily dominate in the remaining districts and to win control of the legislative body.

Packing the opposition's voters into as few districts as possible has the added advantage of reducing overall voter turnout in these areas in the general election since there are few, if any, competitive local races. After all, if the candidate of a particular party is expected to always win by an overwhelming margin, the individual voter has less incentive to vote. Low turnout in these districts means fewer votes for that party's statewide candidates. This effect is especially noticeable in predominantly Hispanic areas and helps explain the historically low voter turnout in these areas.

A third and common tactic of gerrymandering is literally to do nothing. If a party's incumbents prevailed in the latest election, why redistrict even though required by law? The effect is to leave a significant inequality among voters in the districts and to benefit incumbent politicians. This tactic was prevalent in Texas until the 1960s. It is no longer practicable in the United States because, if a state legislature fails to redistrict in a timely manner when a population imbalance exists, a federal court will do it for them. Nevertheless, the tendency to minimize changes is still common in state legislatures, including that of Texas, and is a guiding principle for plans adopted by federal courts.

For many decades, the design of electoral districts unequal in persons (population inequality, or malapportionment) was a common and effective means of limiting the voting strength of opposition political groups in Texas. By overpopulating the districts likely to be won by the opposition and underpopulating the districts likely to be won by members of the dominant political group, the finite number of voters likely to support the dominant political group could be maximized. This form of gerrymandering resulted in a vote in one district or region being of greater or lesser weight than a vote elsewhere and was particularly effective against fast-growing urban centers. It ended in the 1960s with the federal court's requirement for equal population among districts.

At-large or multi-member districts can submerge a political minority, including members of a political party, within a district in which the majority of voters are polarized against the minority. In such districts, the candidates favored by the polarized majority always win all the seats. A fairly drawn single-member system allows some members of the minority groups to elect candidates of their choice. At-large and multi-member districts are not unconstitutional per se, but single-member congressional districts have been required by federal law since 1967.

Both dominant political parties in Texas have engaged in the tactics of gerrymandering and voter repression. Two recent examples illustrate the practice.

As the Anglo Democrats saw minority and Republican voting strength increase around them, they engaged in gerrymandering congressional and state legislative districts in an effort to hold back change and to protect Anglo Democratic incumbents. It was like trying to hold back the sea as wave after wave of change buffeted the institutions that were once the Anglo Democrats' sole proprietorships. Their final stand came in 1991 when the Democrat-controlled legislature passed redistricting plans that gerrymandered district boundaries to aid in the election of African American and Hispanic candidates, while also giving each Anglo incumbent a district in which they probably could win election. Unfortunately for the Democrats, the plan produced bizarre urban districts that the federal courts found objectionable

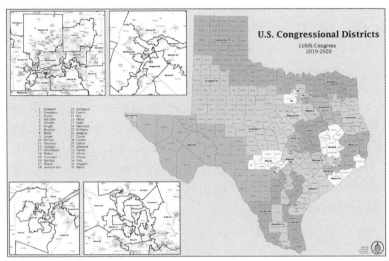

Congressional districts can be bizarre in shape. The outline of a district may have resulted from official policy, such as the Voting Rights Act. In other instances, the peculiar form was the consequence of purely partisan gerrymandering.

and a rationale for Republicans to use for their masterly gerrymandering of congressional districts in 2003.

Republicans used their newfound legislative dominance to draw districts designed to defeat Democratic incumbents and to elect as many Republicans as possible. For example, in the first elections after the 2011 redistricting, Republicans won 69.5 to 72.2 percent (25 of 36 seats in 2012, 26 of 36 in 2014) of the state's seats in Congress while winning only about 58 to 60 percent of the vote in congressional districts statewide. It is surprising that the Democrats received as much as 40 percent of the total vote in congressional races given the low voter turnout in the overwhelmingly Democratic districts. This same dynamic seemed to have less of an effect on turnout in overwhelmingly Anglo districts.

Democratic voters won overwhelmingly (60 to 95 percent) in eleven districts, but probable Republican voters were spread so that they constituted a majority in each of the remaining twenty-five districts. This tactic proved successful in 2012 and 2014. However, spreading probable Republican voters in this fashion was, as described above, a risk. In 2018, two Republican incumbent congressmen were defeated by Democrats in districts thought to have a Republican majority. Another six won reelection by less than five percent. Overall, elections in 2018 resulted in the defeat of eleven Republicans in the state House. At least five Republican congressmen from Texas announced their plans to not seek reelection in 2020.

The composition of current congressional districts in Texas illustrates how gerrymandering is embedded in the state's structure.

CHAPTER 2

IS GERRYMANDERING LEGAL?

GERRYMANDERING IS PRIMARILY ABOUT POWER. One group or party dominates governmental decision-making and wants to retain it by maintaining or enhancing its percentage of representatives. Gerrymandering is one means by which it may control the constituency of electoral districts to ensure that the persons who have the best chance of winning are those who support the group or party in power.

Gerrymandering is also about political survival, especially for individual politicians. A decision about whether to use only single-member electoral districts, how many seats to allocate to a multi-member district, how to shape a particular electoral district, or whether to make any changes at all may be perceived by a politician as crucial to his or her ability for winning reelection. Few politicians are willing to forego the opportunity to affect these decisions.

Gerrymandering further can involve a clash of ideas. An incumbent or party in power feels that their ideas are best and that gerrymandering is justified to ensure they remain in office or power to further those ideas. This concept is contrary to democracy. In a representative democracy, the ultimate judge of the merits of an idea is its acceptance or rejection by the voters through their elected representatives. Any effort to stifle, direct, or manipulate that voting through gerrymandering to bolster an initiative or policy is not justified. But the question remains: Is it legal?

EQUALIZING POPULATION AMONG DISTRICTS

The main function of redistricting in every state is to equalize population among districts. All Texas constitutions have required that seats in the House of Representatives be apportioned among the counties based on a subset of their population. This apportionment was to be "as equal as may be." However, none of them specified the degree of equality that was required. Over time, the electoral districts became increasingly malapportioned.

The US Supreme Court's requirement for equality in population among congressional and state legislative districts set off the so-called "reapportionment revolution" in the 1960s. A significant misunderstanding about voter equality among congressional electoral districts is that this requirement applies only within a state, not nationwide. Therefore, although each of the congressional districts in Texas is equal in the number of persons (698,488) based on the 2010 national census, the number of persons in a congressional district in Texas is not necessarily equal to the number of persons in congressional districts in other states. This imbalance among districts in different states is due to the apportionment of seats in Congress to each state based on its population, with the guarantee that the voters of each state elect at least one member to the US House of Representatives regardless of population.

The 2020 census data was not available at the time of this writing, but the 2010 census and 2011 apportionment of seats is instructive. In 2011, seven states had only one representative after apportionment. In each of these states, the representative is elected statewide; thus, the population of the state is the population of the district. As a result, although the average population of congressional districts nationwide was 710,716 persons according to the 2010 census, and congressional districts are required to be as equal as practicable in population within each state, there was (and will be in 2021) a wide disparity in district population among the states.

The least populated state according to the 2010 census was the statewide district in Wyoming (568,300, including persons overseas). The least populous congressional districts, however, are in Rhode Island. With a total resident population of 1,052,567, the state had sufficient population in 2010 to be apportioned two districts, with approximately 526,283 people in each one. By contrast, the most populous district is Montana, with 989,415 residents according to the 2010 census. Unfortunately for the state, Montana had more than enough residents in 2000 and 2010 for one congressional district but too few (1.4) for two districts. These requirements were part of the compromise between large and small states in the US Constitution.

Allegations of impermissible population deviation were critical to cases in Texas in the 1960s and '70s. Significant allegations of population inequality, however, were absent from most of the litigation in the subsequent decades, except in the challenge to the "mid-decade" redrawing of congressional districts in 2003. Since 1981, due to the stricter standard for congressional districts, congressional plans in Texas have avoided allegations of inequality because the plans consisted of districts that were essentially absolutely equal in population within Texas based on the latest federal decennial census.

State legislative plans since 1981 have remained below the 10 percent total maximum deviation that is generally applicable to non-congressional plans, with senate plans typically having a total maximum deviation of less than 5 percent. The total maximum deviation for a redistricting plan measures the difference between the most populous and least populous districts. It is the measure usually used by governments and courts in the United States because it measures the difference in voting strength between voters at the two population extremes of a plan. In most countries, however, deviation is measured from the norm, average, or quota for a jurisdiction. Thus, a 10 percent deviation in most countries is generally equivalent to a 20 percent deviation in the United States.

In 2011, the senate, House of Representatives, and congressional districts as enacted by the Texas Legislature met the applicable standards of population equality. Indeed, the senate districts had essentially no deviation. It is possible in 2021, however, that allegations about population inequality will reemerge. Even more important, however, it now appears likely that an issue in 2021 and afterward will be whether to continue to use total population as the measure of equality among districts or to use some other measure, such as citizen population, number of eligible voters, or citizen voting age population (CVAP). The ramifications of such a change are enormous, and the legal hurdles are substantial.

FIGHTING GERRYMANDERING IN THE COURTS

Since the legal parameters that define redistricting are rather vague, it can be difficult to prove that a district is gerrymandered. Any definition of gerrymandering is almost meaningless considering the difficulties of proving the purpose behind district boundaries or reallocation decisions. Almost any district configuration or allocation can be justified by ostensibly neutral factors or criteria even if the real purpose is political. This fact does not make gerrymandering appealing or seen as serving the public interest. Rather, it emphasizes the importance of making certain that those persons entrusted with the authority to allocate seats or redraw electoral districts are qualified and free from self-serving or political motives. The Texas Legislature has done many worthwhile things, but in the areas of voting and redistricting its history is characterized by voter suppression and political gerrymandering by the dominant political group. Some political groups have been intentionally shut out of the political system altogether.

Members of the Texas House of Representatives are elected for two-year terms. Texas senators are elected for four-year terms. Senate terms are staggered so that essentially half of the senate districts hold senate elections every two years. However, after each apportionment, a "new" senate is elected. Elections are held in all thirty-one senatorial districts and the senators draw lots during the first days of the next regular legislative session to establish the staggering of terms by determining whether the winner in a district will serve an initial term of two or four years.

The congressional district boundaries in Texas typically have been drawn to satisfy the incumbent member of Congress elected from the existing district. Sometimes, such as in 1965 and 2003, they have been drawn for partisan advantage over an incumbent. Texas has received at least one additional seat in Congress for all but two decades since 1846. It has become almost a tradition in Texas for the boundaries of these new districts to be drawn to favor the election of certain incumbent state legislators.

Although districts have at times been purposely drawn for some state legislators, these legislators have sometimes lost. Circumstances varied in each decade. Sometimes there was no clear advantage to any particular incumbent state legislator because several legislators were interested in possibly running for election in the same new congressional district and their conflicting interests neutralized the line-drawing process. On other occasions, however, it was generally conceded at the time that the boundaries of the new district were being drawn with an incumbent state legislator in mind.

Since the legislative body could not be trusted to act in the interest of neutral democratic voting practices, it was up to the courts to change the system. Courts have been critical to the history of redistricting in Texas. Virtually every Texas redistricting plan in the past sixty years has been challenged in court. The first challenge to the legality of Texas elections came as early as 1873. Most of the litigation has come under the Voting Rights Act of 1965, but almost every case involved some aspect of racial or partisan gerrymandering. The cases were often appealed and remained pending for years. I was frequently on the front lines of trying these cases in Texas, and the process could unfold in any number of directions.

THE ROLE OF THE FEDERAL COURTS

Until the mid-1960s, the federal courts held back from considering legal challenges to congressional or state legislative districting plans. Even when states failed to redraw their congressional seats or to comply with state constitutional provisions requiring periodic redistricting of state legislative seats, the federal courts refrained from considering whether such inaction amounted to invidious discrimination under the United States Constitution. The Supreme Court affirmed this "nonjusticiability" of redistricting plans in 1946 (*Colegrove v. Green*). In his opinion for the Court, Justice Felix Frankfurter asserted, "Of course no court can affirmatively re-map the . . . districts so as to bring them more in conformity with the standards of fairness for a representative system." He would be proven wrong!

When the US Supreme Court in 1962 (*Baker v. Carr*) reversed *Colegrove* and found the constitutionality of districting plans justiciable, many federal district courts remained tentative about using this newly explained authority. Some even expected the Supreme Court to reverse course when it realized the destabilizing effect of the *Baker* decision.

Lawsuits were filed shortly after *Baker* in at least thirty-four states, including Texas, challenging existing congressional and state legislative district plans.

The Supreme Court under Chief Justice Earl Warren did not back down. Eventually, the federal courts became accustomed to considering the legality of districting plans and even to "re-mapping" the state. The evolution of the role of federal courts is demonstrated by the cases in Texas. In the first cases, in the 1960s, the federal district courts moved cautiously, often leaving unconstitutional state enactments in place temporarily for upcoming elections. By the 1970s, however, courts in Texas were willing to substitute a court-approved plan for an unlawful one drawn by the legislature or LRB. These multiple lawsuits in federal court involved the legality of statewide apportionments or the enforcement of Section 5 of the Voting Rights Act, so they were required by federal law to be heard by three-judge courts composed of two federal district judges and one federal court of appeals judge. Any appeal from a decision of these three-judge district courts is made directly to the US Supreme Court.

Since the 1970s, congressional or state legislative elections in Texas have taken place for all or part of every decade using district boundaries drawn or adopted by a federal court. A federal court draws or adopts redistricting plans as needed to ensure that the primary and general elections can go forward if the state institutions, including the state courts, are unable or unwilling to do so in a timely manner. For the next redistricting process in Texas, this means that the state institutions effectively have until the end of 2021, or very early in 2022, to adopt and implement lawful plans redistricting the state's congressional, state House of Representatives, state senate, and State Board of Education districts. Otherwise, the federal courts will do so.

Given the importance of this historical role for federal courts as the architects of congressional and state legislative districts in Texas, it is not surprising that various parties in the past have rushed to find a favorable court forum to hear their case. One lawsuit was filed as early as December 2000, in anticipation of challenging any state congressional redistricting plan that might subsequently be adopted by the legislature in 2001. The lawsuit was filed even before the census had been released showing that the existing districts were malapportioned and needing to be redrawn. A similar rush can be expected to find friendly state or federal forums for challenging any congressional or state legislative redistricting plans adopted in 2021.

The 2010s brought many changes, with federal court rulings that emasculated parts of the Voting Rights Act and suggesting the possibility of redistricting on the basis of citizens instead of population. The 2021 redistricting promises more activity in federal court.

THE ROLE OF TEXAS STATE COURTS

Texas courts never officially saw challenges to redistricting enactments as beyond their jurisdiction. Nevertheless, during the first half of the twentieth century, the state courts did little to alter the redistricting process for state or local governments. There were only a few notable exceptions. A classic case was the occasion when the Texas Supreme Court had to amend the legislative redistricting plan in 1922 to add Swisher County to a House of Representatives district because the adopted legislation had left the county out of any district.

The Texas Supreme Court has held that state district courts have jurisdiction over the constitutionality of redistricting plans. In 1971 and 1981, it nullified redistricting plans for the Texas House of Representatives because the plans violated the Texas Constitution but left the task of coming up with an acceptable plan to the legislature or the Legislative Redistricting Board.

The Supreme Court of the United States determined in 1993 that federal courts must defer to state courts, just as to state legislatures, to come up with a permissible redistricting plan in ample time for upcoming elections. The Texas Supreme Court has opened the door to litigation by making clear that the lawfulness of redistricting plans is justiciable in the state courts and that state courts have the power to remedy unlawful situations, including an invalid redistricting plan. Plaintiffs have tried in at least two decades to get state courts to adopt state redistricting plans. In both the 1990s and 2000s, various plaintiffs rushed to Texas state courts in ultimately unsuccessful efforts to get a favorable state court ruling or order. For various reasons, none of these efforts has produced a final state apportionment plan.

Forum-shopping among the courts can be anticipated in 2021. Attorneys for the two major political parties and most major activist groups may already be scoping the state and federal courts and planning their strategy. A case challenging a state's redistricting is not ripe for filing, however, until the state institution responsible for redistricting (i.e., the legislature or the LRB) either adopts a plan or fails to do so.

EFFECTS OF RACIAL AND ETHNIC DISCRIMINATION AND THE VOTING RIGHTS ACT OF 1965

From its earliest days of colonization by Europeans, Texas has been an area with huge cultural differences among its inhabitants. The State of Texas has never been homogeneous. Sometimes these cultural differences have erupted into open conflict or have been the basis for invidious racial or ethnic discrimination. These differences have played a major role in the state's redistricting experience over the past 184 years and remain important today.

The record of Texas since 1836 is rife with examples of official and unofficial discrimination against African American, Native American, and Hispanic residents of the state. Much of this discrimination came at a time when the Democratic Party had absolute dominance over state and local offices and institutions. Unlawful discrimination continued after Republicans became dominant.

Allegations of racial and ethnic discrimination pervaded past court challenges to this state's districting plans. Attorneys representing organizations such as Mexican American Legal Defense and Educational Fund (MALDEF), National Association for the Advancement of Colored People (NAACP), Southwest Voter Registration Education Project, and the GI Forum played a major role in litigation that opened political processes to minority voters. Among these attorneys are Joaquin Avila, Gary Bledsoe, Nina Perales, Ed Idar, and José Garza. In many instances, the litigation challenging those plans was initiated because of such allegations. The first such lawsuits claimed that the plans were invidiously discriminatory in violation of the United States Constitution, but later cases centered on the Voting Rights Act of 1965, which became a major tool for challenging Texas redistricting plans.

Initially, the Voting Rights Act did not factor heavily in Texas redistricting. Section 2 of the act generally proscribed discrimination against non-white voters and was applied nationwide but was interpreted to encompass the same proscriptions as the Constitution itself. On the other hand, Section 5 of the act applied to only a few states and imposed the extraordinary requirement of federal approval or "preclearance" for a state's election changes, including redistricting. Texas was not subject to Section 5 of the act when it was passed in 1965.

With passage of the Voting Rights Act, the focus shifted from constitutional challenges to the review process under Section 5 of the act by the United States Department of Justice

(DOJ) or a district court in the District of Columbia before any redistricting plan in certain "covered" states could become effective. This process became known as preclearance. This preclearance process applied to all election-related changes adopted by state or local governments anywhere in any of the states or areas covered by Section 5 of the Voting Rights Act. The states in which such preclearance became necessary in 1965 were Alabama, Georgia, Louisiana, Mississippi, South Carolina, and Virginia.

The DOJ could block any new redistricting plan if the covered jurisdiction was unable to show that the plan had neither the "purpose" nor the "effect" of discriminating against one of the protected groups, including black, Native American, or "language" (Hispanic, Asian) minorities. (The 1975 amendments to the act are the origin of the requirement that certain jurisdictions must provide election materials in the minority's language, such as the requirement for election materials in Spanish in Texas.) By blocking the new plan, the DOJ opened the door for courts to adopt their own redistricting plans if the state did not act in a timely manner to correct the legal deficiencies of the blocked plan.

Texas became subject to Section 5 of the Voting Rights Act in 1975. Persons and groups concerned about racial and ethnic discrimination were very effective from 1975 to 1991 in convincing the DOJ to withhold preclearance of parts of Texas's state legislative and congressional redistricting plans and, by doing so, to leave these plans legally unenforceable. The effect was to create a void that was filled by the federal courts, which then adopted or drew redistricting plans designed to remedy the alleged discrimination. By contrast, the DOJ, under the administration of George W. Bush, was generally less responsive to these persons and groups but did object to certain Texas House of Representative districts in 2001.

The role of the Department of Justice under Section 5 was particularly controversial during the 1980s and 1990s.

Although the DOJ denies that it ever had any policy of using the Section 5 review process to "maximize" racial and ethnic voting strength, the agency's actions largely had this effect. By requiring that covered jurisdictions prove that no districting plan had a purpose or effect of discriminating against racial or ethnic minorities, the DOJ essentially compelled covered jurisdictions to adopt the alternative most advantageous to the minority or face the prospect that the entire redistricting plan would become legally unenforceable. In 1995, the Supreme Court criticized the DOJ's conduct and later severely restricted the "purpose" prong of Section 5. Congressional amendments to Section 5 in 2002 were intended to restore the purpose prong of the review process.

Several states and local governments, including those in Texas, challenged the constitutionality of Section 5 of the Voting Rights Act. These challenges bore fruit in 2013 when the Supreme Court struck down the formula that determined which states or areas were subject to the Section 5 preclearance requirement. This decision, *Shelby County v. Holder*, effectively ended the preclearance requirement.

However, Congress in 1982 had amended Section 2 of the Voting Rights Act so that it became a new tool for challenging redistricting plans nationwide. The amendment addressed the possibility that Section 2 merely repeated the proscriptions of the United States Constitution. Congress imposed a new requirement applicable nationwide that "no voting qualification or prerequisite to voting or standard, practice, or procedure shall be imposed or applied . . . in a manner which results in a denial or abridgement of the right of any citizen of the United States on account of race or color" or membership in a "language minority." It was no longer necessary to demonstrate that a challenged plan was enacted with a discriminatory purpose. Section 2 remains a potent tool for challenging discriminatory redistricting plans.

Ironically, along with aiding Democrat-leaning racial and ethnic minorities in Texas, the Voting Rights Act generally benefited Republican candidates. The process of drawing districts with African American or Hispanic voting majorities made those districts heavily Democratic, given the tendency of these minority voters to support Democratic candidates. By concentrating these reliably Democratic voters in heavily minority districts, however, they become unavailable to provide Democratic majorities in surrounding districts. Thus, drawing heavily minority districts necessarily increased the percentage of non-Hispanic white voters in the surrounding districts.

Many Hispanic persons consider themselves within the "white" classification and answer accordingly on the census. Thus, a more accurate term to use to describe the category of persons referred to as Anglo in the early stages of colonization is "non-Hispanic white." In most circumstances, an increase in the percentage of non-Hispanic white voters in a district means that the district is then more likely to vote for a Republican candidate. As a result, state legislative and congressional districts in Texas have generally become more clearly Republican or Democrat in part because of the Voting Rights Act.

Statewide election results seem to confirm this effect. Competitive legislative or congressional districts in which candidates from either party might prevail have become less common. However, Democratic victories in predominantly non-Hispanic white "Republican" state House of Representative districts and Republican victories in predominantly Hispanic congressional and state House districts apparently showed that there were, in fact, more competitive districts than previously supposed. The earlier Republican victories over Democratic incumbents in some of these districts can be seen either as anomalies or as cases in which the districts remain competitive because a significant portion of the voters in these districts are not locked into support of a candidate because of party or racial or ethnic label. This latter possibility is supported by the results of the 2018 election, when Democrats won several congressional and state legislative districts in which the majority of voters were non-Hispanic whites and Republicans continued to prevail in some predominantly Hispanic districts.

COURT CHALLENGES TO PARTISAN GERRYMANDERING

Allegations of partisan gerrymandering appeared in the litigation of the 1960s and have reappeared in every subsequent decade. These allegations, however, never prevailed. For the first four decades, it was Republicans who claimed that the state's redistricting plans impermissibly discriminated against them. In the 2000s, especially after the congressional redistricting of 2003, and in the 2010s, it was the Democrats who alleged that the redistricting plans were partisan gerrymanders in violation of the United States Constitution. The Democrats lost their claims, too. Recently, the US Supreme Court found in *Rucho v. Common Cause* that partisan gerrymandering is not justiciable in federal court.

Although the legal challenges were lost, there are many examples from Texas's past in which both major political parties used their control of the legislative redistricting process to favor the party in power or certain incumbents.

BURDENS OF PROOF

Generally, the burden of proof and burden of persuasion rest with a person challenging a state enactment, including a redistricting plan. In other words, the state enactment is assumed to be valid unless the plaintiff can show otherwise. Redistricting litigation, however, is filled with circumstances in which this usual dynamic is directly altered or where the plaintiffs can easily shift the burdens to the state.

In challenges under the Fourteenth Amendment to the equality in population of state legislative and congressional redistricting plans, plaintiffs can meet their burdens by showing an excessive level of population deviation among the districts. At this point, the burden shifts to the state to show justification for such deviations. When the first lawsuits were filed in the 1960s, the disparity of population among districts was so great that no justification could suffice. Under the law today, a state bears the burden of specifically justifying any deviation in a congressional district from absolute equality. Effectively, there appears to be virtually no justification allowable for any deviation in the population of congressional districts within a state. As a result, Texas congressional districts are now all drawn so that they are within one person of the ideal population according to the most recent decennial census.

For state legislative and state board of education districts, however, the so-called "10 percent rule" for a total maximum deviation has meant that the state did not need to justify deviations within this range. This rule for years provided essentially a "safe harbor." Recent federal decisions suggest that Texas should no longer assume that state legislative districts can avoid an equal population challenge if they have a total maximum of less than 10 percent. The state should have adequate, objectively verifiable justifications for any population deviations, including for state legislative districts.

The burden may also readily shift in challenges to Texas House of Representatives districts under Section 26 of the Texas Constitution. Once a showing is made that a substantial number of county boundaries have been cut in the apportionment plan, the state must justify each cut by showing that it was authorized by Section 26 or was necessary to meet requirements of federal law. In Texas cases during the 1970s and 1980s, the state House of Representative plans were nullified in their entirety because the state plan extensively cut county boundaries with insufficient justification for such cuts.

The clearest example of a difference from the normal allocation of burdens occurred under Section 5 of the Voting Rights Act before it was effectively nullified by the US Supreme Court in 2013. Any change in an election practice or procedure in a covered jurisdiction, such as a redrawing of state legislative or congressional districts, had to be precleared before it could become effective. The burden in this preclearance process was placed by law on the "covered jurisdiction," such as the State of Texas, to show that this change was not for the purpose, nor would it have the effect, of denying or abridging the right to vote of the protected racial or language minorities. Over the past four decades, the State has on many occasions failed to meet this burden to the satisfaction of the US Department of Justice. Under Section 2 of the Voting Rights Act, the burden is placed on the plaintiff.

COMPLEXITY OF VOTING RIGHTS LITIGATION

Redistricting litigation is complex. In some instances, the cases have required trial over several days with many parties, attorneys, and witnesses participating. The plaintiffs have come variously from the Democratic Party, the Republican Party, Associated Republicans of Texas, NAACP, MALDEF, GI Forum, Southwest Voter Registration Education Project, League of United Latin American Citizens (LULAC), members of the state legislature, private groups, and various local governments and officials.

It is interesting to see how the political changes in the state are reflected in the juxtaposition of the various interests in litigation over the decades. Persons or organizations challenging redistricting plans in one case, or decade, sometimes found themselves on the opposite side at other times. This was also true for the state itself. As the domination of one political party or group in the state legislature or the state's elected offices (especially attorney general) declined or grew, organizations or persons previously appearing as plaintiffs or plaintiffs' counsel began appearing on the side of the state, or as state's counsel, and vice versa. In many instances, these individuals, groups, and interests ended up in a single case once the various lawsuits were consolidated and the interventions were allowed.

Since individual state officials sometimes intervened and took radically different views of the legality of different plans, it was difficult to identify who properly constituted "the state." The Texas attorney general is responsible for representing the state in such litigation in defense of state law, but in some circumstances the authority or intentions of the attorney general to act on behalf of the state to negotiate or present redistricting plans in a judicial setting have been questioned by other state officials as motivated by partisan bias.

Attorneys have assumed a unique importance in developing redistricting strategy and in the initiation and prosecution of redistricting cases. Many of the same attorneys appear and reappear over the decades generally advising and representing the same organization or interest. In most circumstances, the attorneys were the real strategists and movants behind the litigation, while the individual plaintiffs or intervenors were incidental to the filing and progress of the cases. In some instances, the success or failure of a group can be traced to the experience of the group's attorney in prior redistricting cases.

THE NATURE OF VOTING RIGHTS LITIGATION

There are primarily two types of witnesses in voting rights litigation: politicians and "experts" (usually political scientists).

The politicians or legislative staffs are "fact" witnesses who testify to the circumstances of enactment of the redistricting plan and possibly the policy or purpose behind the districts in the plan. I am always apprehensive about presenting politicians because the very traits that make them successful in politics, such as self-confidence and talkativeness, sometimes make them terrible witnesses on cross-examination. The best politician witness in my experience was Lt. Governor Bill Hobby before the federal court in 1981. He was subjected to intensive and sometimes rude cross-examination. At one point, Federal Judge Barefoot Sanders looked over at me and seemed to question with his eyes why I did not object to how Hobby was being treated. I signaled that I was not going to intervene. I could tell that Hobby knew he was doing well. He was having fun.

On the other hand, the need to cross-examine political witnesses can sometimes result in conflicting situations. Jim Nowlin was presented as a witness for Republicans challenging the 1981 redistricting. He had left the legislature and had been appointed federal judge. I had had and later would have many cases before Judge Nowlin. Nevertheless, I found myself aggressively cross-examining him in his role as a witness.

"Expert" witnesses usually submit a report and testify as to why a redistricting plan is or is not discriminatory. These witnesses are hired by the different parties for their testimony and, not surprisingly, often have differing views one from another, especially about voter polarization, after looking at the same evidence. This tendency for political scientists to reach different conclusions on review of the same election results is one reason why I view such testimony with skepticism. I have always enjoyed the task of studying expert witness reports for flaws and cross-examining such witnesses in depositions and at trial. Some do well; some implode on the stand.

For example, the predominantly Anglo and wealthy City of Kingwood in northeast Harris County sued the City of

Houston to stop the latter from annexing it. Kingwood hired one of the best and most expensive law firms in Houston. The City of Houston hired me and my law partners because Kingwood was asserting the unique argument that the annexation was invalid under the Voting Rights Act since Kingwood was racially polarized. Voter polarization is customarily shown through a regression analysis in which the vote for or against a candidate is compared to the racial or ethnic makeup of election precincts in the jurisdiction to measure the correlation of the two. The firm acting for Kingwood hired a well-known political scientist as its witness to prove its case. I reviewed the witness's report. I did not disagree with his conclusion that Kingwood voters were probably biased against minority candidates, but there was something about the report that did not seem right.

After I spent the first day of trial generally probing the witness's methodology, his mistake became apparent. I waited until the second day to expose it. When I began my examination on the second day, the federal judge warned me that he was not in the mood for a lot of technical questioning about the expert's report. I started my questioning by referring the witness to the official election returns in Kingwood for a specific statewide election and pointed out that it showed a certain candidate received 1,022 votes in a certain precinct. I asked how many votes were used for his expert report. He checked on the data on that computer printout and answered "twenty-two." I could hear the groans of Kingwood's attorneys.

I repeated the sequence of questions for another candidate in another precinct where the official returns showed 299 votes; only ninety-nine were used in the report. The expert had not realized that the computer program was written to drop all but the last two digits in a precinct's total vote. At this stage, the courtroom doors opened, and my intern entered pushing a dolly stacked high with boxes of election returns. I told the judge that they would all show that the expert had done his analysis using only the number of votes corresponding to the last two digits of the actual returns. "The report is worthless," I claimed. Kingwood's attorneys asked for a recess. They later withdrew the report and the judge dismissed the lawsuit.

So much for high-priced lawyers who know little about voting-rights litigation and high-priced "expert" witnesses who are too arrogant to check the accuracy of their own reports.

THE ROLE OF JUDICIAL PARTISANSHIP

Some attorneys insist that the greatest predictor of the outcome in a redistricting lawsuit is the partisan affiliation of the president who appointed the judges hearing the case. The history of redistricting in Texas contains some litigation that supports this claim and some that does not. Are judges impartial in redistricting cases, or do they rule according to political biases? A starting point is to understand what is meant by "impartiality." Justice Scalia expressed his view, in his majority opinion regarding *Republican Party of Minnesota v. White*, as follows:

> One meaning of "impartiality" in the judicial context— and of course its root meaning—is the lack of bias for or against either party to the proceeding. Impartiality in this sense ensures equal application of the law . . .
>
> A judge's lack of predisposition regarding the relevant legal issues in a case has never been thought a necessary component of equal justice, and with good reason. For one thing, it is virtually impossible to find a judge who does not have preconceptions about the law . . . . Indeed, even if it were possible to select judges who did not have preconceived views on legal issues, it would hardly be desirable to do so. "Proof that a Justice's mind . . . was a complete *tabula rasa* in the area of constitutional adjudication would

be evidence of lack of qualification, not a lack of bias . . . "
[authority deleted]

A . . . possible meaning of "impartiality" . . . might be described as open-mindedness. This quality in a judge demands, not that he have no preconceptions on legal issues, but that he be willing to consider views that oppose his preconceptions, and remain open to persuasion, when the issues arise in a pending case. This sort of impartiality seeks to guarantee each litigant, not an equal chance to win the legal points in the case, but at least some chance of doing so.

From my experience, judges in redistricting cases generally start with preconceptions about the fairness or legality of a plan. For some attorneys, the trial and briefing are merely a means by which to provide the judge ample justification for his or her probable result. The job of the attorney is to develop and pursue the best strategy for winning in front of each judge. It serves no purpose for an attorney to gripe or complain because the presiding judge is conservative or liberal, Republican or Democrat, or to blame an unfavorable outcome on the partiality or political mindset of the judge.

Over sixty-five years ago, in *Colegrove v. Green,* Justice Frankfurter observed that if the legality of redistricting plans became justiciable in federal courts, those courts inevitably would be drawn into the "political thicket" of election contests and "the politics of the people." Frankfurter proclaimed, "It is not less pernicious if judicial intervention in an essentially political contest be dressed up in the abstract phrases of the law." He warned that court involvement in this political thicket ultimately would affect the public's perception of the integrity of the courts. Some think that this in fact has happened, given the public's often cynical view about the rulings of courts in redistricting plans.

As will be shown in subsequent chapters, courts have played a major role in opening the political process in Texas to groups and political parties that had previously been shut out. Their efforts, however, have been tremendously uneven. Partisan gerrymandering by the legislature and the legal response of the courts have shaped who gets to hold power in Texas.

CHAPTER 3

THE LONG REIGN OF TEXAS DEMOCRATS (1836–1960)

THE ORIGIN OF THE LONGSTANDING dominance of Texas Democrats can be found in the particular racial demographics of Texas in the nineteenth century and the chronic conflict and shaky legal truces among native populations, Hispanic settlers, Anglo settlers, and African Americans. The battles fought and revolutions launched were multifaceted and had profound effects on the way borders were drawn and populations defined—all of which impacted the work of redistricting and seeded the gerrymandering that would follow.

The key point to note—as Texas independence was forged, as the state was annexed into the United States, when it seceded with the Confederacy and was then readmitted to the Union—is that the democratic system was drawn by Anglos. The six Texas constitutions followed Anglo political methodology and traditions and were written in the English language. While there were occasional surges in minority representation in Texas state government, ultimately Anglo

Democrats seized power and held it, ensuring that government gridlock around redistricting would protect their hegemony. It is in this period as well that pitched battles between the legislature and courts slowly determined in what circumstances gerrymandering was legal or illegal, setting the stage for the many controversies in the twentieth century that inform our present moment.

THE TEXAS CONSTITUTIONS: PROVISIONS ON SUFFRAGE AND APPORTIONMENT

Texas had six constitutions from 1836 to 1876. All six of the Texas constitutions contained provisions governing apportionment of state legislative seats. Five themes affecting redistricting dominated these provisions: definition of elector (i.e., who can vote); a requirement for periodic enumeration of "inhabitants" or "electors"; reapportionment of the senate and House of Representatives following this enumeration; the utilization of counties as the basic building blocks for electoral districts; and districts of contiguous territory. No Texas constitution, however, prescribed either standards or procedures for drawing congressional districts.

The largest impact of each constitution on redistricting had to do with which people were defined as qualified electors. The first three of the constitutions prohibited slaves ("and their descendants"), Indians, and women from becoming electors eligible to vote or to hold office. The attitude toward Indians was summed up by L. D. Evans, who was chairman of the committee of the 1845 convention charged with determining the amount of public land in Texas. In his report to the convention, he urged, "[D]espoil the Indians of this country whenever it shall be needed for the occupancy of civilized man." Most land inhabited by Indians was considered public land. There was no provision in these constitutions expressly barring Spanish, Mexican, or Hispanic persons from being citizens and voting, but there was little, if any, effort to encourage or even to accommodate their vote or participation in the government.

There were numerous reasons for the limited political participation of Hispanics. First, the sparsity of the Hispanic population in Texas and its concentration in the remote southern part of the Republic caused the group to be largely overlooked by Anglo immigrants. Second, there was considerable distrust by Anglos of all Hispanics, which led to violence on occasion; lynching of Hispanic "troublemakers" was common. Third, some Anglos feared that the Hispanics in Texas were conspiring with Mexico to recapture the state. Frequent raids by troops and outlaws from Mexico fed this fear. Some Anglos sought and killed innocent Tejanos in retaliation. Finally, the previous Spanish governmental structure was one in which leaders were not generally elected. As a result, few Hispanics had experience with elections or seeking elective office.

The difference in language was a further impediment to the Hispanic participation in the political process. Rule in an "unknown tongue" was a reason given in the Texas Declaration of Independence as a reason for independence from Mexico. Most political documents and election information were in English. Few Hispanics of the era spoke, wrote, or read easily in English.

Largely Hispanic South Texas lacked educational institutions, whereas education was buttressed in the Anglo communities, teachers and schools were welcome, and many older students were sent "back east" to continue their education. Anglo Texas had one of the highest literacy rates in the world. At the same time, among Hispanics, only the rich landowners had the capability to educate their children. The first feeble attempts at a statewide public education system did not emerge in Texas until almost 1870.

Introduction of an unfamiliar form of government made active participation in politics difficult and confusing for many Hispanics. Spanish and later Mexican governments were organized around municipalities, with each area dominated by its largest municipality through an *ayuntamiento* (council) that usually was not elected. One of the first acts of the new Republic of Texas, however, was to begin creating and defining the borders of counties, which were a form of government to which the Anglo colonists were accustomed. With the defining and subsequent organization of these counties came sheriffs, justices of the peace, constables, and representatives to the new Republic's Congress. At least initially, these offices were not necessarily filled by election as much as by designation or by voice vote in local meetings to which few Hispanics were invited or in attendance.

By 1845, there were approximately thirty-seven counties, each with at least one representative in the Texas Congress. When counties began to be formed in South Texas, the local Hispanics were seldom the founding influence. Although few American settlers lived in San Antonio or South Texas even after the war with Mexico, many European immigrants settled there. Germans in particular were attracted to this part of Texas.

From their first immigration to Texas in the 1830s, the Germans tended to cluster in ethnic enclaves. A majority settled in a broad, fragmented belt across the south central and southwest regions. Germans soon constituted the third largest national-origin group in the state. Like their Anglo neighbors to the north, they helped organize counties in South Texas and became the state representatives, sheriffs, and judges of the new counties. This German influence remains today. For example, the 1990 United States Census showed that 1,175,888 Texans claimed pure and 1,775,838 partial German ancestry, for a total of 2,951,726, or over 17 percent of the state's total population.

There were only two counties in the mid-1880s in South Texas, Bexar and San Patricio, and thus little or no representation in the Texas Congress. Bexar County was created in 1836 for all western and South Texas, including parts of the future states of New Mexico and Colorado. Bexar County was represented in the 1845 Constitutional Convention by one delegate, José Antonio Navarro, the only person among the sixty delegates with a Spanish surname. The major policy issues, such as annexation by and, later, secession from the US, stirred great animation among the Anglos but little enthusiasm among Hispanics, who felt powerless to affect the outcome. Hispanic turnout was low in elections.

Many Hispanics in South Texas remained as much a part of Mexico as of the Republic of Texas, or later the United States. They freely crossed the Rio Grande and spent time both north and south of this border. The overall effect, even if unintended, was to suppress Hispanic participation in the politics of the Republic and new state. Hispanics could vote and were eligible to hold office, but few sought election even in the new counties, especially after the Republic of Texas was annexed by the United States. Some of these factors, and their residual effects, remain significant today.

THE CONSTITUTION OF THE REPUBLIC OF TEXAS (1836)

Independence from Mexico of the Republic of Texas was declared on March 2, 1836. The Constitution for the new republic was drafted by a convention of fifty-nine delegates who assembled at Washington-on-the-Brazos on March 1, 1836. The new constitution was approved by the Constitutional Convention on March 16 and by a popular vote in September of that year.

The Constitution of 1836 defined citizens of the Republic as "free white persons" and provided that "All persons, Africans, the descendants of Africans, and Indians excepted" who were residing in Texas on the day of the Texas Declaration of Independence "shall be considered citizens of the Republic, and entitled to all the privileges of such." Theoretically, this wording might have allowed white women to vote, but there is no indication that it was intended to do so or that any women tried to vote.

The Texas Constitution provided for an enumeration of citizens every four to eight years with the reapportionment of seats in the House and redistricting of the senate after each enumeration. The enumeration excluded "Africans, descendants of Africans, and Indians." This provision of exclusion was comparable to Article II, Section 2, of the US Constitution excluding "Indians not taxed" from the federal decennial census and considering only three-fifths of an area's "non-free persons" for the purpose of apportioning seats in Congress. However, Texas excluded Africans and their descendants altogether from the numbers used for apportioning seats in the Texas Congress, thus advantaging counties with primarily farmers and farmland rather than plantations.

Senators were to be chosen in districts "as nearly equal in free population (free negroes and Indians excepted) as practicable." One senator was elected from each district. The House of Representatives consisted of twenty-four to forty members apportioned among counties roughly according to the number of electors within each county, with each county entitled to at least one representative. In a county apportioned two or more seats, the elections were held at-large with the county acting effectively as a multi-member district.

THE CONSTITUTION OF THE STATE OF TEXAS (1845)

As a condition of the admission of Texas as a state in the United States, Texas had to submit for approval by federal authorities a new constitution. This constitution was adopted by Texas in 1845. Only one Hispanic, José Antonio Navarro, was among the sixty-four delegates who signed the document. Qualified electors of the State of Texas were defined to include every "free male . . . (Indians not taxed, Africans, and descendants of Africans excepted)" who was a citizen of the United States or the Republic of Texas. Originally, the provision read "free white males," but the word "white" was stricken by amendment during the convention.

The number of state legislators was expected to grow but, after considerable debate and amendment, the Constitutional Convention could not agree on a formula for determining the respective size of the senate in relation to the House. Instead, it combined counties to form nineteen senate districts to exist for at least four years until an official enumeration of electors was taken. Further, it provided for the future that the senate shall never be less than nineteen nor more than thirty-three members.

The Convention also prescribed the number of representatives for each county, from one to four. There were thirteen single-member districts and twenty-three multi-member districts. This allocation of seats was to last until an enumeration was taken. The total number of representatives was sixty-six for thirty-six counties. Despite its size, Bexar County received only two representatives. For the future, the constitution provided that the legislature would prescribe the number of representatives "according to the number of free population in each, and shall not be less than forty-five, nor more than ninety." By limiting the basis for redistricting to "free" persons, counties with large slave populations were limited in representation compared to counties with little or no slave population.

This range in the number of state legislators allowed the size of both chambers to be enlarged by the legislature in the future as the number of electors in the state increased. The constitution specified that members were to be apportioned among the counties. Senate districts were created using whole counties. If a senatorial district consisted of two or more counties, it could not be separated by a county in another district. In other words, the districts must be contiguous.

On becoming a state, Texas was apportioned two congressional seats in the US House of Representatives and two US senators. The representatives were elected, while the senators were appointed by the Texas Legislature. In 1848, the Texas Legislature added flotorial districts to the mix of single-member and multi-member districts. Flotorial districts are electoral districts that are a combination of counties that also elected other representatives with one or more counties represented only through the flotorial district. They can effectively submerge and minimize the voters that are only in the flotorial district. For example, consider a large county whose population would be sufficient for six-and-a-half districts, while an adjacent small county might have enough population to constitute only one-half of a district. The larger county would elect six representatives from a multi-member district. The large and small county together would constitute a flotorial district that would elect one representative. The voters in the larger county could overwhelm the voters in the smaller county, giving the larger county control over the outcome in seven representative races.

Texas often used flotorial districts throughout its history—until declared unconstitutional in 1964—but not necessarily for the purpose of discrimination. New apportionment bills

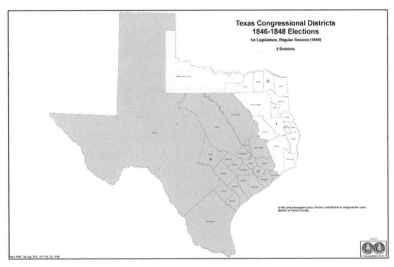

The two congressional districts in Texas in 1846 to 1848, after annexation by the United States. The counties then created were nearly all in East Texas or along the coast. Bexar County stretches throughout West Texas. San Patricio County encompasses South Texas.

were routinely enacted during this period as the population and number of House members grew.

THE CONSTITUTIONS OF THE STATE OF TEXAS (1861 AND 1866)

The constitution approved by the 1861 Constitutional Convention, called together in response to the election of Abraham Lincoln, was largely the same as the 1845 constitution. In most instances, the wording of the Texas Constitution of 1845 was kept intact, but the words "United States of America" were replaced with "Confederate States of America." A clause of the 1845 constitution permitting the emancipation of slaves was eliminated and the freeing of slaves was declared illegal. The new constitution called for an enumeration of "free inhabitants" and generally apportioned the state representative districts according to free population among counties, but with House districts "nested" inside the senate districts. Thus, each of the senate districts had one or more of the House districts within its border, with multi-member elections in House districts where any county had more than one representative. This pattern of having House and senate districts coterminous continued until changed by the 1876 constitution.

As the Union Army expanded its occupation of much of the Confederacy, slaveholders in those areas often moved their slaves to Texas to avoid having them emancipated. By 1865, there were an estimated 250,000 slaves in Texas. Then, although the Confederacy had lost the Civil War, President Andrew Johnson's Reconstruction programs allowed the states of the Confederacy, including Texas, to reenter the Union with few penalties.

The post-war Texas Constitution of 1866 was drafted primarily by Confederate veterans. It no longer contained provisions approving slavery, but it continued to define an elector as a "free male" and excluded "Indians not taxed, Africans and descendants of Africans." Moreover, the constitution proclaimed, "No person shall be a representative unless he be a white citizen of the United States." A similar provision applied to the senate. There are no Hispanic surnames among the delegates to the constitutional convention.

This constitution required an enumeration of all "inhabitants (including Indians taxed)" in 1875 and every ten years thereafter, with apportionment of the seats of the legislature following the enumeration. It continued the apportionment of seats from 1860 "until changed by law." Texas sent a delegation of senators and representatives to Congress, but the delegation was turned away by a Congress now firmly under the control of the "Radical Republicans."

THE CONSTITUTION OF THE STATE OF TEXAS (1869)

As shown by the 1866 constitution, some Anglo Texans were reluctant even after the end of the Civil War to grant equal rights to the African American inhabitants of the state. Although slaves had been freed, their rights to vote and hold office remained curtailed. This soon changed.

So-called Radical Republicans in Congress took control of Reconstruction after the mid-term elections of 1866. In 1867, President Johnson was impeached. Johnson was acquitted in the US Senate by one vote, but he lost the ability to influence or to shape Reconstruction policy. In that same year, Congress removed civilian governments in the South and placed the states of the former Confederacy under the rule of the US Army. Persons who had held leading positions under the Confederacy were temporarily denied the vote and were not permitted to run for office.

Rule by the Union Army brought many changes in Texas. J. W. Throckmorton, a Unionist, had been elected governor of Texas in 1866, but he clashed often with the Union Army commander, General Philip Sheridan. In 1867, Sheridan removed Throckmorton and other state officials from their positions.

A new constitutional convention was mandated by the US military. However, although it was in session for over 150 days in 1868–1869, the convention accomplished little and was beset with resignations and expulsions. One major point of controversy was whether former Confederates should be allowed to vote or hold office. There were ten black delegates, five of whom protested that the adopted provisions were too lenient on these former Confederates and unfair to "loyal" Americans who had never stopped believing that the US Constitution was the law of the land. At least one of these protesting African Americans, George T. Ruby, resigned, saying that the convention was "lost" and that "its continued session will only terminate in disgrace to the entire country." Among the other African American delegates at the Convention were Benjamin O. Watrous, Benjamin Franklin Williams, and Stephen Curtis. There apparently were no Hispanic delegates.

The convention adjourned without approving a final document. A resolution in the final days read as follows:

> Thus, that inasmuch as this Convention has been in session over one hundred days, and has not as yet made anything like a Constitution under which the people can live, therefore, Be it resolved, That this Convention do adjourn on Thursday, the fourth day of February, 1869, at twelve o'clock, noon, and that this adjournment be *sine die*, never to assemble again.

This resolution failed to pass, but three days later the convention essentially dissolved as it lost its quorum and adjourned. The military governor was left to finish the job. Reportedly, military officers gathered the available materials and published the Texas Constitution of 1869.

This new Texas Constitution granted full rights of citizenship to African Americans but not to women. It delineated the specific counties for each of the state's senate districts. The House electoral districts continued to be "nested" within the senatorial districts and the number of representatives (two to four) elected to the House of Representatives in each senate district. The senate and House districts were to remain in effect until changed by law. The districts were to be reapportioned after each federal decennial census.

Unlike the earlier 1866 congressional delegation from Texas, this one was seated by Congress. There were four congressmen: three Republicans and one Democrat. Both US senators were Republican. This Republican success was short-lived, as it depended largely on former Confederates not voting.

After Republican governor E. J. Davis lost the 1873 election, Democrats dominated elective offices in Texas, including the governorship, for the next 105 years. In 1952, the Texas

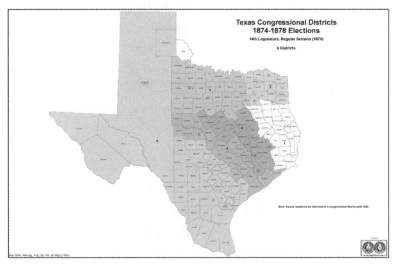

The six congressional districts in Texas, 1874 to 1878. One stretches from South Texas to the Panhandle. Also shown are the counties recognized by this time. Most of West Texas and the Panhandle remained unorganized. South Texas remained underpopulated.

Republican Party nominated mostly Democrats—including Allan Shivers, who was the incumbent governor and the Democratic nominee—so that they appeared on the ballot as both the Democratic and Republican nominee. It is probably correct to assert that it was 109 years after E. J. Davis's election in 1869 (or 105 years after he left office) before another Republican became Texas governor, since "Democrat" Shivers beat "Republican" Shivers by 1,375,547 to 468,319 votes. The next Republican to become governor was Bill Clements, who won election in 1978 and took office in 1979.

THE CONSTITUTION OF THE STATE OF TEXAS (1876)

The current Constitution of Texas was adopted at a constitutional convention in 1875 after the end of congressional reconstruction and took effect in 1876. Three delegates were elected from each of the state's thirty senatorial districts. Seventy-five members were Democrats and fifteen, including six African Americans, were Republicans. One African American member was legislator David Abner, who later was vice president of the 1876 Republican State Convention. He was also one of only three African Americans in the Fifteenth Legislature (1876). Shortly after the convention convened, one of the African American Republican members resigned, and his place was taken by a white Democrat. None of the delegates in 1875 had been in the 1869 convention. There were no women or Hispanic delegates. About forty delegates were members of Grange, an agricultural and rural public interest organization.

Article III, Section 2, of the 1876 Texas Constitution provides that the senate shall consist of thirty-one members. The House of Representatives, which consisted at the time of ninety-three members, is limited to a maximum of 150 members. Article III, Section 25, of the constitution requires that senatorial districts must be contiguous, with the election of one senator from each of thirty-one districts. At the time of adoption, senate districts were to be "as equal as may be" in the number of "qualified electors." Until amended in 2001, each senate district was to be based on the number of "qualified electors." The section is now silent on this point.

A new senate is elected after each reapportionment. All senate seats are filled at the next general election, with the elected senators then drawing lots in the next legislative session to determine the staggering of the senators' four-year terms. As adopted, Section 25 of the constitution allowed only one senator for any county regardless of the county's population. This last provision severely restricted the representation of fast-growing urban counties such as Harris and Dallas.

Under Article III, Section 26, of the 1876 constitution, the House election districts are required to be apportioned among the counties according to population "as near as may be," with any county of sufficient population entitled to a representative. The Section sets out a formula for when two or more counties may be joined to form a representative district and when a county boundary may be split to remove "surplus population" from one county to constitute part of a district. Section 26 has been the subject of significant litigation, as discussed elsewhere in this book.

This constitution returned the state to a mix of single-member, multi-member, and flotorial districts, which remained in use until the 1960s. As adopted, Article III, Section 28, of the 1876 constitution required that "at its first session after publication of each United States decennial census," the state legislature must "apportion" the state in accordance with the provisions of Article III, Sections 25 and 26.

AFRICAN AMERICANS EMERGE AS A POLITICAL FORCE IN THE REPUBLICAN PARTY

Once enslaved and denied citizenship, male African Americans were now entitled to full citizens' rights. During the period from 1866 to 1870, the Thirteenth, Fourteenth, and Fifteenth Amendments to the US Constitution were ratified to abolish slavery, to ensure that anyone born in the US was a citizen, and to prevent the denial of the right to vote to any (male) citizen based on race, color, or previous condition of servitude. States that had been in the Confederacy had to ratify these Amendments as a condition of their readmission to the Union. Foremost among the new rights extended to African Americans was the right to vote. There were over 200,000 former slaves in Texas, many of whom fled the state; the remaining 70,000 were now potential voters with considerable potential clout.

Initially, the African Americans who remained in East Texas expected plantations to be split up and the land given to the former slaves. When this did not happen, many African Americans moved to cities such as Beaumont–Port Arthur, Dallas, and Houston. Most African Americans in Texas turned to the Republican Party. They owed their freedom to the success of the Union Army and the politics of the Radical Republicans. Soon, the new African American voters made up a majority of the radical wing of the Republican Party.

Many African Americans were active in the Republican Party leadership, among them a vice president of the Republican State Convention, delegates to the National Republican Convention, a national committeeman from Texas, and members of the state Party's Executive Committee. The legislature of 1870 had Republican majorities in both the Texas Senate and House of Representatives, including two African American senators and eleven African American representatives (given that there were no more than ninety-three state representatives at the time, this figure was proportionately greater than exists today). Republicans held three of four congressional seats. A major African American leader during this period was Norris Wright Cuney, who in 1886 served as a committeeman for the National Republican Party.

After 1875, the percentage of African Americans in the Texas Legislature and in local elections declined. Even within the Republican Party their influence became less, as the "lily whites" gained ascendancy over the African American faction of the party. Rejected by Anglo Republicans and Democrats, African American voters sometimes turned to third parties, such as the populist People's Party, but most African Americans remained in the Republican Party. In fact, most African Americans who had joined the People's Party found their way back to the Republican Party after the former's demise.

THE DEMOCRATS SEIZE CONTROL

Republican success waned when the former Confederates regained the right to vote and organized as Democrats. As the nineteenth century progressed, a phenomenon occurred similar to one to be seen in Texas in the 1980s, when the conservative wing of the Democratic Party morphed into the core of the Republican Party. Here, conservative Anglo Republican voters and officeholders increasingly fled the Republican Party and aligned themselves with the Democrats, eventually constituting the conservative core of the Democratic Party of the late nineteenth and early twentieth centuries. This development ensured the dominant position of the Democrats.

Republican candidates consistently lost elections in this era. Nevertheless, in 1897 there was still at least one African American Republican in the Texas Legislature. Robert Lloyd Smith served in the Texas House of Representatives (1895–1897, leaving office in 1899). By the start of the twentieth century, however, there were no African Americans, Hispanics, or Republicans in the state legislature. (This is true of the Texas Legislature in 1901, but a few Republicans can be found among the chamber's members in subsequent years. A few Mexican Americans were legislators from 1876 to 1883 but only occasionally thereafter. Representative José T. Canales of Brownsville served in five legislatures from 1905 to 1919, but only one or two other Mexican Americans were elected before 1930.)

Between the years 1901 (when Robert B. Hawley finished his second US House term) and 1954 (the seating of Bruce Alger), the sole Republican to represent Texas in Congress was Harry M. Wurzbach, who served in the US House for most of the 1920s, leaving office in 1931. The Democratic Party's rule was essentially absolute at the state and local levels in Texas. In most counties, victory in the Democratic primary amounted to election to the office.

VOTING DISCRIMINATION AGAINST AFRICAN AMERICANS AND HISPANICS

Voting discrimination against African Americans and Hispanics persisted in the first half of the twentieth century. Although Texas did not require people to pass a literacy test to register as voters, it levied a poll tax, had miscegenation laws, required separation of races on public transportation and related facilities, mandated separate public schools, and required property ownership for voters in some elections. These restrictions fell disproportionately on racial and ethnic minorities. Even when these laws did not explicitly apply to Hispanics, they were often a factor, along with separate schools and the lack of Spanish-language election materials, in keeping Hispanics segregated and not voting.

Total voter participation dropped markedly in Texas in the early 1900s, essentially ending Republican and Populist competition and leaving elections to be dominated by Anglo Democrats. The state's introduction of a poll tax was a major cause of this decline because it effectively kept many poor minorities and Anglos from voting.

Since African Americans were voting primarily Republican at this time and were ineffective at challenging the Democrats' dominance in the general election, the Democrats took steps to keep them from affecting the Democratic primary. Initially, the policy of excluding African Americans from the Democratic primary was local. However, a statute passed in 1923 provided: "[I]n no event shall a Negro be eligible to participate in a Democratic Party primary election in Texas."

This statute and the policy it embodied was challenged in federal court in a series of cases known as the "white primary cases." After the statutory wording was struck down by the US Supreme Court in 1927, the executive committee of the Democratic Party adopted similar wording. In 1932, this action was struck down. The Democratic Party of Texas state convention then adopted a rule banning African Americans from voting in Democratic primary elections. This revised scheme was upheld by the federal courts on the basis that the political party was a private entity. The US Supreme Court reversed this position in 1944, and Texas white primaries were found unconstitutional. However, it was not until 1952, after five trips to the United States Supreme Court, that the vestiges of this blatantly discriminatory policy were finally clearly forbidden—a good test case as to how arduous it can be to fix voter discrimination through the courts.

In addition, the state relied on at-large or multi-member elections for state representative elections during the late nineteenth and early twentieth centuries. Although the purpose may have been benign, an effect of these elections was to submerge the voting strength of racial, ethnic, and political minorities (i.e., Republicans) in an Anglo Democratic voting majority. During the first half of the twentieth century, at-large elections also became common in cities and school districts. There were some legitimate reasons for preferring at-large or multi-member elections to a single-member or ward system, but the effect of these local systems was also to submerge racial, ethnic, and political minorities.

APPORTIONMENT GRIDLOCK AND GERRYMANDERING

During the nineteenth century, the legislative and congressional power of Texas resided almost exclusively with rural Democratic legislators elected from the northeast, central, and eastern coastal parts of the state. These were the areas that had been first settled by immigrants from the United States and that remained the most populous areas of the state during most of the nineteenth century. Much of West Texas at this time continued to consist of less populated areas that had not yet been organized as counties.

Over time, however, this situation changed. The inhabitants of Texas and new immigrants to the state from the United States and other countries increasingly moved into the underpopulated areas. For example, between 1910 and 1920, the population of the counties in the high plains of West Texas increased almost fivefold, and the population of Hidalgo and Cameron Counties in South Texas tripled, while counties in Northeast and Central Texas grew slowly or even lost population. New counties were created, but the West and South Texas areas remained underrepresented in the Texas Legislature.

Urban areas, such as Dallas and Harris Counties, grew rapidly. These and other urban areas also were underrepresented in the state legislature. As a result of population growth elsewhere in the state, the East and Central Texas legislators found their legislative dominance and even reelection in jeopardy. Nevertheless, the Texas Legislature continued to reapportion after each federal decennial census through the nineteenth century. This result was made possible in part because of Article III, Section 25, of the Texas Constitution that limited a county to a single senator and by the ability of the legislature to gradually increase the number of state representatives from 93 to 150 (the limit was reached in 1921), allowing incumbent legislators to keep their seats by adding new legislative seats elsewhere in the state as a response to demographic changes. Eventually, these means of more or less preserving the political status quo were exhausted or became insufficient.

The legislature's failure to pass a senate apportionment in 1911 was the first outward sign of an approaching legislative gridlock. In 1911, the 32nd Legislature, 1st Called Session, passed a senate apportionment bill, which the governor vetoed. This decision possibly was affected by the fact that the state's urban voters were underrepresented in the legislature but were important in statewide elections, such as for governor. Subsequently, senate reapportionment was not addressed until 1921, when it was taken up by the 37th Legislature, 1st Called Session, following the 1920 census. In 1931, the legislature failed to pass legislation redrawing either House or senate districts.

In 1936, an amendment was adopted to the state constitution adding Article III, Section 26a, which limited a county to a maximum of seven state representatives. This provision was subject to an exception that if a county exceeded 700,000 in population, it was entitled to an additional state representative for each additional 100,000 in population. Although this new provision was clearly intended to limit the number of representatives in urban counties, some people hoped that Section 26a would encourage the legislature to get back to the business of redistricting. It did not. The legislature remained gridlocked.

This gridlock was in effect a status quo gerrymander intended to benefit incumbents and the more rural areas in East and Central Texas that had more representatives than their population justified. Since existing district lines worked to the incumbents' advantage, those with the power to change them had no incentive to do so.

CONGRESSIONAL DISTRICTS: STATEWIDE ELECTIONS

A pattern in Texas's drawing of congressional districts developed in the late nineteenth and early twentieth centuries. This pattern had two parts. First, the state steadily grew in population. In fact, the state's apportionment of seats by Congress increased each decade with the federal decennial census, except in the 1920s when Congress could not agree on an apportionment of congressional seats, and in the 1940s when Texas grew more slowly than the nation as a whole. Second, new seats were initially elected statewide.

Why statewide elections? There were no incumbents in these new districts to guide the drawing of the district boundaries. By allowing these new seats to be filled in a statewide election before a district was drawn, the legislature avoided picking a winner or part of the state in which to put any new district. By allowing these new seats to be filled first, there would be incumbents by the next legislative session. These statewide elections also virtually ensured that the new members of Congress would be chosen by Anglo voters who constituted a clear majority of statewide voters. The state had only two congressional districts in 1846 and four districts by 1866. Given two new seats in 1870, the Texas Legislature initially kept the lines of the four existing districts and elected the two new members of Congress statewide.

By 1874, the legislature had drawn six districts. Anti-Hispanic bias seems to have affected the drawing of these early congressional districts, as shown in 1874 to 1878, when a single district encompassing the heavily Hispanic South Texas stretched northward to the Panhandle and included Anglo-populated counties to the east. No Hispanic won election to Congress until Henry B. González in 1961. The number of congressional seats increased to eleven by 1882 and to sixteen after the 1890 census. Because the legislature was unable to agree on a redistricting plan after the 1910 census until 1917, the new congressional representative was elected statewide until the legislature eventually agreed to the configuration of eighteen single-member districts. Congress failed to reapportion seats among the states in the 1920s, so Texas did not redraw its existing districts.

When Texas was apportioned three new seats in 1931, these seats were filled in 1932 by statewide elections. In

1933, the legislature successfully enacted a plan that included twenty-one single-member districts. The districts remained unchanged after the 1940 census. Because the legislature was unable to agree on a plan after the 1950 census, the state's new congressional seat was left to be elected statewide until twenty-two districts were drawn in 1955. The new congressional seat apportioned to the state after the 1960 census was again initially elected statewide.

MALAPPORTIONMENT

Through the first half of the twentieth century, population disparities grew in Texas's congressional and state legislative districts. Article III, Section 25, of the Texas Constitution, which limited counties to a single senator, and Section 26a, which limited a county to no more than seven representatives, provided official exceptions to the more general state constitutional requirement for equality in population or electors, but the disparity in population also grew among state legislative and congressional districts not directly affected by these constitutional exceptions. For example, from 1874 to 1930, the ratio between the most populated and least populated congressional districts hovered between 1.3 and 1.9 to one. However, once Texas effectively delayed drawing its congressional districts after 1934, the disparity climbed to 3.6 to 1 by 1950 and to 4.4 to 1 according to the 1960 census.

Similar gross disparities in population also grew in the state legislative districts. For example, in 1950, Harris County had only eight state representatives when, based on its population, it was entitled to fifteen.

ABSOLUTE ANGLO DEMOCRATIC DOMINANCE

The Democratic Party's rule of statewide, congressional, and legislative elections over the period 1873 to 1960 was essentially absolute. Only a few exceptions existed. Republican congressman Harry W. Wurzbach (Seguin) won election to Congress in 1920 and was reelected multiple times, dying in office in 1931. Republican Bruce Alger of Dallas served in Congress from 1955 to 1965. One Republican shows up in the House for 1903, two in 1905 and 1907, and three in 1909. For the next sixty years there was only one Republican at most in the Texas House, and for thirty-two of those years there were none. In the senate, Republicans were even rarer. A single Republican, Julius Real of Kerrville, served six years (1909–1915) and then was elected again for four years (1925–1929), but the next Republican senator would not appear until 1967. The key word for all these Republican victories is "isolated."

Racial and ethnic minorities also had limited electoral success. No African American from Texas served in Congress or in the state legislature from 1899 until the 1970s. Hispanics achieved only slightly greater success. By 1961, there had been a handful of successful Hispanic candidates for the Texas House of Representatives (six were serving in 1961 out of 150 House members) and Henry B. González had won election first to the state senate (1956) and then to Congress as a Democrat in a 1961 special election. However, the election of González was an exception. Domination of the elections by the Democratic Party during this period generally meant rule by conservative, non-Hispanic white Democrats.

Even with control of the redistricting process held by a single wing of one political party, the process was acrimonious. For example, the *San Antonio Express* described some of the early twentieth century plans as "political and geographical freaks" that were the product of "selfishness and prejudices."

TEXAS COURTS

Although Texas courts did not adopt a formal "political question" doctrine like their federal counterparts, they were largely able to sidestep the legal issues posed by state legislative redistricting (or the lack thereof) and the malapportionment that resulted. An exception was in 1922, when the Texas Supreme Court was needed to put a county (Swisher) into a state legislative district plan after the legislature mistakenly left it out (*Smith v. Patterson*).

By contrast, the Texas courts during this period often assessed the legality of the redistricting of county commissioner precincts. While stopping short of "redoing" the precincts themselves or requiring counties to redistrict because of malapportionment, the courts imposed certain standards for redrawing commissioner, justice, and election precincts, such as requiring that they must be "in good faith and without fraud, not arbitrary, nor in gross abuse of discretion." One court even indicated that the precincts could not be drawn for the purpose of providing representation according to race without regard to population or other permissible factors. Another cautioned against drawing precincts for the benefit of one set of persons to the detriment of the people.

CREATION OF THE LEGISLATIVE REDISTRICTING BOARD

The Texas Legislature in 1947 attempted to end the redistricting gridlock by adopting a joint resolution proposing to amend Article III, Section 28, of the Texas Constitution to provide for a Texas Legislative Redistricting Board to redistrict the state legislative districts if the legislature failed to do so in its first regular session after release of the federal census. The amendment was approved by the voters but did not become effective until 1953, so it did not apply when the federal census arrived in 1951. Nevertheless, the Texas Legislature for the first time in thirty years redrew state legislative districts following the 1950 census, but without solving the problem of malapportionment.

The LRB has become a stage for high-profile political battles. Some of the past battles have been partisan, such as when one or more of the members were from different political parties or different wings of the same party. Others, though, were the result of intra-party maneuvering by board members to test who was best positioned to run for higher office. The LRB is composed of five of the top state officials, including four elected statewide. Almost all have their eyes on higher office.

The audience with the greatest immediate interest consists of the affected legislators whose redrawn district boundaries may mean the survival of the incumbent and reelection for as long as the next decade. LRB members are in the prized position of deciding for or against political groups or individual incumbents. This gives LRB members considerable political leverage, especially if they can prevail in their position on the board (three votes) with which to win the allegiance of affected legislators for the LRB members' future plans.

Pertinently, and as previously noted, the LRB lacks authority to redraw congressional districts.

FEDERAL COURTS: THE REAPPORTIONMENT REVOLUTION

In a watershed case in 1946, the United States Supreme Court declined to review allegations of vote dilution caused by the failure of state legislatures to follow constitutional mandates for periodic redistricting. A majority of the court found such issues to be a "political question" nonjusticiable in federal court (*Colegrove v. Green*).

In 1960, however, the United States Supreme Court laid the foundation for its later decisions allowing challenges to redistricting plans and explicitly protecting the electoral rights of racial minorities in the "redistricting" context. In 1960, the court permitted a lawsuit to proceed in federal court that challenged the attempt by the Alabama Legislature to redraw the municipal boundaries of the City of Tuskegee to remove the largely African American areas, such as Tuskegee Institute, from the City. A majority of the court saw this local law as "districting" legislation that, if plaintiffs could prove their claims, constituted an effort to keep African Americans from voting in city elections, a denial of the right to vote in violation of the Fifteenth Amendment, and not a political question (*Gomillion v. Lightfoot*).

It may seem strange that I devote only this single chapter to over 100 years of Texas history. Much, of course, happened over this period, but in terms of the subject of this book, the 100 years was a period of little change. The dominant culture was Anglo, and the dominant political party was the Democratic Party, which was committed to retaining political power. Efforts to redistrict frequently stagnated into inaction that maintained the Democrats' power. By 1960, however, the stage was set for the federal courts to mandate major changes in the Texas election system.

CHAPTER 4

REAPPORTIONMENT

REVOLUTION

(1961–1970)

THE 1960S BROUGHT MONUMENTAL CHANGES to the legal requirements for Texas redistricting. The Texas congressional, House
of Representative, and senate districts were badly malapportioned by 1960. As described in the previous chapter, the legislature had failed to comply with the Texas constitutional
requirements that state legislative districts be "as nearly as
may be" equal in population (House of Representatives) or
electors (senate).

The Texas Legislature was not alone in its violation of
state constitutional requirements for periodic reapportionment of legislative districts of equal population. The problem
was nationwide. Generally, both federal and state courts did
nothing to correct such state legislative inaction.

In *Colegrove v. Green* (1946), a majority of the United States
Supreme Court, led by Justice Felix Frankfurter, rejected
federal court intervention to remedy the situation, reasoning
that redistricting or reapportionment was "a political thicket" of party interests, party contests, and political questions

that were not justiciable in federal court. Some observers, however, saw the *Colegrove* decision as indicating a divided court that might reach a different conclusion in the future. In the years following the *Colegrove* decision, the US Supreme Court had numerous opportunities to become involved but, often on procedural or equitable grounds, avoided the substantive questions surrounding the justiciability of reapportionment plans.

The prevailing view on the US Supreme Court changed dramatically by 1962. A majority of the court in *Baker v. Carr* narrowed the concept of "political question" and held that a claim that a redistricting plan is unconstitutional because invidiously discriminatory can be decided by the federal courts. *Baker* opened the doors of federal courts nationwide but provided little insight into the standards or principles that the Supreme Court would ultimately apply to congressional and state legislative redistricting.

Federal district courts struggled with their newfound authority. Some lower-court judges even thought that the Supreme Court would back away from its decision in *Baker* when given another chance. Within nine months, lawsuits were pending in federal courts in at least thirty-four states challenging existing state legislative or congressional districting plans or both. Many of these lawsuits quickly found their way to the United States Supreme Court by direct appeal from the three-judge federal courts that were required in statewide apportionment cases.

Cases involving congressional and state legislative redistricting plans were argued before the Supreme Court in November 1963. The court ruled on congressional districts first. In *Wesberry v. Sanders*, the court found that Article I, Section 2, of the United States Constitution imposes a requirement that congressional districts within a state must be as equal in population as practicable. Equality of population in the districts within a state is required even though the disparity in the population of congressional districts may vary enormously among the states.

Many of the lawsuits from around the nation challenging state legislative districts were consolidated at the Supreme Court. In a series of decisions released simultaneously in 1964, the Supreme Court effectively struck down existing state legislative districting plans nationwide by ruling that both houses of a state legislature must reflect "the fundamental principle of representative government in this country [of] equal representation for equal numbers of people" (*Reynolds v. Sims*). The court resisted the temptation at the time to establish any exceptions, such as allowing states to follow the model of the US Senate that one of two legislative bodies could be based on something other than population (*Lucas v. Forty-Fourth General Assembly of Colorado*).

While the requirement for population equality among congressional districts was based on Article I, which is the part of the US Constitution establishing the House of Representatives, the state legislative cases were decided under the Equal Protection Clause of the Fourteenth Amendment, which is a more general requirement that applies to the states. Because the requirements for population equality arise under different parts of the US Constitution, the court imposed different levels of permissible deviation from precise equality—i.e., virtually no permissible deviation for congressional districts with potentially as much as ten percent total maximum deviation for state legislative districts.

The Texas Legislature did not heed the warning in *Baker* in a timely fashion.

CONGRESSIONAL DISTRICTS

Congressional districts in Texas were particularly vulnerable to a legal challenge based on population inequality. The Texas Legislature in 1961 was unable to agree on a plan redrawing congressional districts. Therefore, the plan used in the 1962 elections was composed of twenty-two congressional districts that still had essentially the same boundaries as drawn by the legislature in 1933, plus the statewide election of the one additional seat apportioned to Texas after the 1960 census. A congressional redistricting plan had been passed in 1957, but the primary boundary change in the legislation was to split Harris County into two congressional districts, thereby eliminating the seat that had been elected statewide since 1952. Otherwise, the 1957 legislation made few changes.

Despite the population disparities evident in the state's congressional districts, the legislature failed in 1961 to act to cure them. The *Baker* decision came down on March 23, 1962. The legislature was not in session. The governor refused to call the Texas Legislature into special session for redistricting. The legislature did not meet again until it came into regular session in 1963. The first lawsuit was filed when the legislature was still in session in 1963. Other lawsuits soon followed.

The primary federal court challenge to the state's congressional districts came in *Bush v. Martin*. The lead plaintiff was George H. W. Bush, head of the Republican Party in Harris County. The named defendant was Texas Attorney General Crawford Martin. In this and the many later cases challenging the state's redistricting, the named defendant was always a state official. Relief was unavailable against the state itself. The named defendant varied, sometimes indiscriminately, among the governor, lieutenant governor, attorney general, and secretary of state.

In 1963, a three-judge federal court struck down the state's existing (1957) congressional apportionment plan because of "spectacular" disparities in population among the districts. It noted that the district containing the Dallas metropolitan area was the most populous congressional district in the nation (951,527). This district in Dallas was an example of

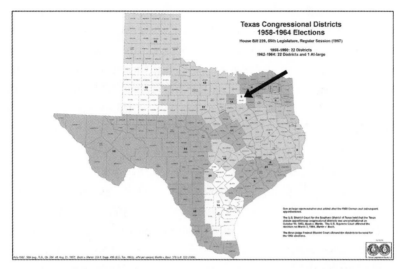

Congressional districts from elections of 1958–1964, with arrow point-
ing to Dallas county

how the shape of an electoral district is not necessarily an
indication of gerrymandering and how a significant deviation in population can be an effective gerrymander.

Situated in the upper center of the Texas map below is
District 5. It is compact, contiguous, and regular in shape and
encompasses only one county, Dallas County. It seems the
perfect non-gerrymandered district. The opposite was true.
Why did this configuration exist? Democrats controlled the
Texas Legislature, but Republicans were becoming stronger,
especially in the Dallas area. The redistricting plan solved
this political problem in part by making Dallas County a
single, overpopulated district. It was a classic case of gerrymandering through packing an opponent's voters into as few
districts as possible—in this instance aided by population
inequality.

The legislature's malign motive for its treatment of Dallas
County was shown by comparison to how it had inconsis-
tently split the state's other large county, Harris (containing
the city of Houston), into two districts. By keeping all of

Dallas County in one district, the legislature limited Dallas Republicans to only a single congressman, denied African American voters in Dallas County an opportunity to elect a person of their choice to Congress, and kept a non-Hispanic white Democrat in office in adjacent District 4.

A majority of the three-judge court (District Judge Joe Ingraham and 5th Circuit Judge John R. Brown) required that all of the 1964 congressional elections occur statewide. District Judge James Noel dissented. He maintained that the use of statewide elections would mean that "not less than 16" of the twenty-three congressional seats would be controlled by the major population centers, such as Dallas and Houston, thereby leaving many of the regions of the state without any representation. The court's plan was stayed by the circuit justice of the United States Supreme Court pending the outcome in *Wesberry v. Sanders*, which was under consideration by the court.

The district court further stayed its order to permit the 1964 election to go forward on the basis of the previous state apportionment, with twenty-two single-member districts and one seat filled by a statewide election. Republican Bruce Alger, who had served as a congressman from Dallas since 1955, was defeated for reelection in 1964. Alger lost in a Democratic wave in Dallas after the Kennedy assassination. Alger was a far-right conservative whose extreme views and antics were blamed by some for Lyndon Johnson's presidential victory in 1964.

In 1965, the Texas Legislature passed a new congressional apportionment plan, but the litigation continued against this new plan, which split Dallas County between two districts, thus eliminating the worst of the malapportionment. The three-judge federal district court acknowledged that the remaining statewide deviation of 19.4 percent in the new plan was too great but considered it "a good faith effort by the legislature toward achieving substantial numerical equality."

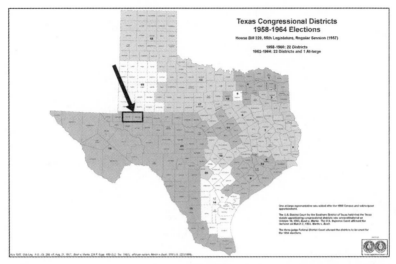

Congressional districts as they existed for the 1962 election, in which Republican Ed Foreman won the far Western district largely because of the vote in Midland and Ector Counties.

The court explained, "Against the past of the long existing discrimination . . . and with corrective legislation coming from an assembly which is itself unconstitutionally constituted, we think there are likewise many reasons why this approval should be tentative and for a limited duration." The court refused a request to allow the plan to be in effect until after the next census in 1970. The legislature passed a new plan in 1967 that was in effect for the 1968 and 1970 elections.

PURGING REPUBLICAN CONGRESSMEN

The litigation in *Bush v. Martin* also is noteworthy because it contained other claims that were a preview of what was to come in later decades. The original plaintiffs had come from Harris County, but many other parties were allowed to intervene. Some of these intervenors alleged that the congressional apportionment passed in 1965 was a "regional gerrymander" discriminating against certain cities, counties, and parts of

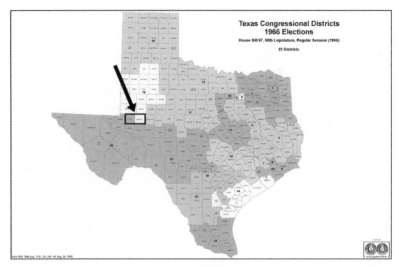

Congressional districts drawn in 1965, with apparent intention to defeat
Ed Foreman in Ector County by splitting Ector and Midland Counties.

the state. The Republican Party alleged that the plan gerrymandered the state to dilute the Republican vote. The court
denied these claims.

In hindsight, it is possible to interpret that the 1965 congressional apportionment plan probably was drawn in part
to defeat a Republican incumbent in the Texas congressional
delegation and to protect Democrats. The Republican incumbent was a young man, Ed Foreman, from Odessa (Ector
County). Foreman's election in 1964 from the district in far
West Texas had been a surprise. The apparent partisan analysis was that Ector County and adjacent Midland County
were hotbeds of Republican voting. If Midland and Ector
counties were allowed to remain in the same district, reelection of Foreman or another Republican was almost certain.

From the Democratic perspective, therefore, the counties
had to be separated (cracked) and put in different districts to
dilute the Republican vote. The 1965 redistricting plan moved
Ector County into a district that was heavily Democratic and
that included San Angelo. Midland County was combined in

a district with Lubbock to the north, which was expected to continue to vote Democrat. This plan was a classic "cracking" gerrymander.

Foreman lost his reelection bid in 1966. Midland and Odessa would not be combined again in a congressional district until 2001, when state representative and later Speaker Tom Craddick insisted on a return to this configuration. On the other hand, George H. W. Bush won election in Harris County in a congressional district (District 7) that packed Republicans. The court's discussion of these various claims in 1965, however, demonstrates the difficulty that has continued to plague all claims of partisan gerrymandering through 2019.

STATE LEGISLATIVE DISTRICTS

The Texas Legislature had redrawn the state legislative districts in 1961, but the plan still had large population deviations. Lawsuits were expected, especially after the Supreme Court's decision in *Baker.*

Several lawsuits came in state court. One lawsuit asked the Texas Supreme Court to withhold the salaries of the members of the Texas Legislative Redistricting Board so long as that body did not correct the population imbalances in the state legislative plans adopted in 1961. A second lawsuit challenged the use of multi-member districts in the state House of Representatives' apportionment plan because such districts violated African American voting rights. The plaintiffs pointed out that no African American had been elected to the Texas Legislature in the twentieth century. Neither of these state lawsuits was successful.

The challenge in federal court to the state legislative district plans came in *Kilgarlin v. Martin.* The case was initiated in July 1963 after the legislature had adjourned. The same three judges who heard *Bush v. Martin* also heard this challenge to the state legislative districts. As with many federal courts nationwide, the federal court in Texas proceeded slowly, waiting for more direction from the Supreme Court. As a result, despite the population disparities evident in the state's legislative districts, the court permitted the 1964 elections to proceed based on the 1961 legislative plans.

In January 1965, after the Supreme Court decision in *Reynolds v. Sims*, the three-judge court entered a summary judgment declaring Sections 25 (limiting counties to a single senator regardless of the county's population) and 26a (limiting counties to seven representatives) of Article III of the Texas Constitution and the 1961 apportionment plans to be in violation of the Fourteenth Amendment to the United States Constitution. The court, however, declined to grant the plaintiffs' request for injunctive relief. Instead, it retained jurisdiction and indicated that, if the legislature failed to enact a valid apportionment by August 2, 1965, the plaintiffs could petition for further relief. The Texas Legislature responded by enacting new state legislative apportionment plans during its 1965 regular session.

The 1965 plan for the Texas House of Representatives was again challenged. The plaintiffs alleged that the House plan invidiously discriminated because of its excessive population deviation (a total maximum deviation of 26.48 percent), its use of flotorial districts, and its alleged use of gerrymanders and multi-member districts to dilute the voting strength of racial and political minorities. The court remained reluctant to intervene in the state's redistricting process and granted only limited relief. The claims of vote dilution were denied, as was the claim of excessive population inequality among the districts. The three-judge court struck down only the flotorial districts.

The US Supreme Court allowed the 1966 elections to go forward on the basis of the 1965 plan, including the flotorial districts. After hearing the case on appeal, the Supreme

Court in 1967 upheld the invalidation of the flotorial districts but also found the other districts in the Texas apportionment invalid because of the statewide total maximum deviation of over 26 percent. The Texas Legislature redrew parts of the apportionment plans in 1967 to eliminate the flotorial districts and again in 1969 to overcome the most egregious population deviations. In subsequent hearings, the three-judge court generally accepted the legislative action as a "good faith" effort to correct the plans' deficiencies but suggested that the population deviations were still too high. The state legislative elections in 1968 and 1970 were carried out using the districts in the legislative enactments.

The court denied the claims of political gerrymandering and the challenge to the multi-member districts. Although unsuccessful in *Kilgarlin v. Martin*, political and racial minorities used the litigation to hone their theories of vote dilution, particularly with regard to the effect of multi-member districts. These theories would bear fruit in the following decade.

THE UNITED STATES SUPREME COURT AND RACIAL DISCRIMINATION

The US Supreme Court's decisions requiring state legislative and congressional districts to be equal in population did not explicitly deal with the discriminatory effect of unequal districts on this nation's racial minorities. These court decisions were basically majoritarian. The "one person, one vote" principle ensures the opportunity of a majority to elect a majority of a legislative body. It was clear, however, that, to the extent the decisions were intended particularly to eliminate discrimination against the underrepresented residents of the nation's cities, the decisions also positively affected the voting strength of the nation's African American population that was growing within those cities.

THE REQUIREMENT OF POPULATION EQUALITY FOR TEXAS COUNTY COMMISSIONER PRECINCTS

The lawsuit that extended the requirement of "one person, one vote" to state political subdivisions began in state court in Texas. The mayor of the City of Midland, Hank Avery, objected to the plan of the Midland County Commissioners' Court that put most of the City of Midland in a single commissioner's precinct. This precinct had an overwhelmingly larger population (estimated at 67,906) than any other of the four precincts. The others, all rural areas, had populations of about 852, 414, and 828 respectively. The Texas Supreme Court found that the plan violated the Texas Constitution but left open the possibility that factors other than the number of voters could be considered in the drawing of commissioner precincts because the work of the county commissioners mostly affected rural areas. Dissatisfied with this ruling, Avery carried his challenge by writ of certiorari (the seeking of a judicial review of a decision made by a lower court or government agency) to the US Supreme Court, which in 1968 held that the county commissioners' plan violated the US Constitution (*Avery v. Midland County*).

EFFECTS

Despite the efforts of the Democrat-controlled Texas Legislature to draw districts in the 1960s to minimize the loss of non-Hispanic white Democratic incumbents in Congress and the state legislature, the effect of the federal court rulings was immediate and substantial. These courts put an end to gerrymandering through malapportionment.

The ruling that Article III, Section 25, (limiting a county to a maximum of one state senator) of the Texas Constitution was invalid effected major changes. Representation from the state's urban areas greatly expanded, especially in Harris and Dallas Counties, with the addition of senate seats in those areas. By the end of the decade, there were two Republicans in the state senate from these areas and one African American, Barbara Jordan.

Republican membership in the House rose to seven after the 1962 elections but dropped to only one after the 1964 election that featured the victory of Lyndon Johnson for the US presidency. The ruling that Article III, Section 26a, of the Texas Constitution (limiting a county to seven representatives) was invalid increased the number of state representatives apportioned to the urban counties, but the legislature's use of multi-member districts in these urban areas continued to stifle the magnitude of the change in political, racial, and ethnic minority representation in the Texas House of Representatives. By the end of the decade, there were still only eight Republicans in the state House of Representatives.

Harris County now had three congressional districts. Many of the identifiable areas of Republican strength in Harris County were packed together in a single congressional district (the 7th). This overwhelmingly Republican congressional district elected future president George H. W. Bush in 1966. Dallas County now had two congressional districts. Also in 1966, the first African Americans in seventy years were elected to the Texas Legislature, including Curtis Graves and Joe Lockridge in the House and Barbara Jordan in the senate.[1] Other people who would later significantly affect

---

1. After unsuccessful campaigns for the Texas Legislature in a multi-member district in 1962 and 1964, Barbara Jordan won a seat in the Texas Senate from Harris County (Houston) in 1966, becoming the first African American state senator since 1883 and the first black woman to serve in that body. She was reelected to a full term in the Texas Senate in 1968 and served until 1972. In 1972, she was elected to Congress, becoming the first woman elected from Texas. In 1974, she played a significant role on the House Judiciary Committee in the potential impeachment of Richard Nixon.

both state and national politics first won election (e.g., Oscar Mauzy and Charlie Wilson) in 1966. All were Democrats.

Republicans had not won an election statewide in Texas since the 1860s. This circumstance changed in 1961 when Republican John Tower won the special election called to replace Lyndon Johnson after the latter resigned to become vice president. Democrats generally considered Tower's victory an anomaly that would soon be corrected. However, Tower won reelection in 1966, 1972, and 1978. Tower opposed the Voting Rights Act and was a strong voice for the South.

Still, Democrats dominated the statewide elections of 1968. In the race for governor, Preston Smith won against Republican Paul Eggers, garnering 57 percent of the vote. However, a few new pockets of Republican voting sprouted. A red sweep in the far north Panhandle produced few net Republican votes because the area was sparsely inhabited but was a harbinger of things to come statewide. Ector and Midland Counties also went Republican. Republican voting strength was apparent in the two most populous counties, Dallas (north central) and Harris (southeast), where portions of these counties voted overwhelmingly for Republican candidates.

CHAPTER 5

URBAN CHANGES
(1971–1980)

DURING THE 1970S, LITIGATION OVER state legislative and congressional districts in Texas resulted in some of the most significant United States Supreme Court decisions of the decade. The Texas Legislature in 1971 again adjourned without fulfilling all its reapportionment responsibilities. It had passed a new plan for the Texas House of Representatives, but the senate districts remained unchanged. A new plan for congressional districts was later passed in a special session.

STATE HOUSE OF REPRESENTATIVE DISTRICTS

The plan for the House of Representatives had been passed during the regular legislative session. Litigation came quickly in state court. Republican State Representative Tom Craddick of Midland and three Republican Party officials challenged the legislature's plan. The plaintiffs' real concern was probably the partisan gerrymandering embodied in the enactment. For example, the conservative Democrat Speaker of the House of Representatives, Gus Mutscher, had been openly accused of vindictiveness in pairing liberal

Democrats and Republican incumbents or putting disliked members in hostile districts. This was the period in which the "Dirty Thirty" (a group comprising both Democratic and Republican legislators) became renowned for posing opposition to the Speaker.

The legal attack, however, focused on how such gerrymandering was achieved through the "wholesale cutting of county lines" (thirty-three cut counties) in apparent violation of Article III, Section 26, of the Texas Constitution. Section 26 generally requires that House districts be apportioned using whole counties and that counties be kept intact whenever possible. The Texas Supreme Court recognized that the strict wording of Section 26 must succumb to the Fourteenth Amendment requirement of population equality but held that Section 26 was not nullified in its entirety. The court expected the state to demonstrate that any county cuts were justified by Section 26 or efforts to comply with the Fourteenth Amendment. The state, however, presented no evidence to meet this burden. The Supreme Court affirmed the lower court's ruling that the legislation was unconstitutional in violation of the Texas Constitution (*Smith v. Craddick* [September 16, 1971]).

Since the legislature had failed to enact legislation redrawing state senate lines, this task fell to the Texas Legislative Redistricting Board pursuant to Article III, Section 28, of the Texas Constitution. With the ruling in *Smith v. Craddick*, however, the question emerged as to what to do about redistricting the Texas House of Representatives. Representative Craddick, a successful plaintiff in the earlier challenge to the House district plan, was probably surprised and disappointed by the answer to that question. Immediately following the ruling in *Craddick*, Democratic senator Oscar Mauzy petitioned the LRB, which was composed of five Democrats, to proceed to apportion the state into representative as well as senatorial districts. The LRB declined on the basis that it had no jurisdiction over the House districts because Article III, Section 28, of the Texas Constitution applied only when the legislature failed to enact reapportionment legislation.

Mauzy immediately instituted a direct action at the Supreme Court asking for a writ of mandamus (a court order compelling the execution of a duty) to oblige the LRB to redraw the House districts. In an opinion that was issued only eleven days after its opinion in *Craddick*, the Texas Supreme Court delivered the requested mandamus (*Mauzy v. Legislative Redistricting Board* [September 27, 1971]). The court, however, rejected several of Mauzy's other requests, including one to bar the LRB from including multi-member districts in its apportionment plans.

Since the House redistricting bill was deemed invalid, the obligation to redistrict the House of Representatives fell to the Legislative Redistricting Board. Now the LRB had jurisdiction over redistricting both the senate and the House of Representatives.

THE LEGISLATIVE REDISTRICTING BOARD

The 1971 LRB consisted of these five state officials: Attorney General Crawford Martin, Lieutenant Governor Ben Barnes, Speaker of the House of Representatives Gus Mutscher, Comptroller of Public Accounts Robert S. Calvert, and Commissioner of the General Land Office Bob Armstrong. The chief justice of the Texas Supreme Court at this time was Robert W. Calvert. He and Robert S. Calvert were unrelated but were sometimes mistaken for each other. The chief justice often joked that whenever he was in the news, the paper would mistakenly run a photo of "that old man," the comptroller. All five LRB members were elected Democrats. Republican representative Craddick's winning litigation had inadvertently tossed the issue of redistricting the House to an all-Democratic body.

Predictably, the LRB adopted redistricting plans that favored the election of Democrats, but it was split about whether to use countywide or single-member elections in the urban counties. Bob Armstrong advocated for single-member elections as an issue of fairness to minority voters and candidates. Lt. Governor Barnes was in favor of countywide multi-member elections. Barnes prevailed.

GRAVES V. BARNES

The LRB released its apportionment plan for the Texas Senate on October 15 and its plan for the Texas House of Representatives a week later. Shortly afterward, four lawsuits, one in each of the four separate federal districts in Texas, were filed challenging the plans. One suit filed in the Southern District alleged that the senatorial districts in Harris County were racial gerrymanders that discriminated against the county's African American population. The lawsuit challenging the senate was filed on behalf of African American representative Curtis Graves from Dallas. The named defendant was Lt. Governor Ben Barnes, who was the presiding officer of the senate. The other three lawsuits attacked the statewide reapportionment plans for the House and senate.

The forums chosen (the Tyler Division of the Eastern District, the Northern District, and the San Antonio Division of the Western District) clearly demonstrated an effort by the plaintiffs to aim for forums they believed would be favorable to their particular claims. The lead counsel for the challenge in Tyler, David Richards, acknowledges that he searched for a plaintiff who lived in Tyler so that he could file his suit before Judge William Wayne Justice. Richards maintains he never met appellee Diana Regester, later named in the case *White v. Regester*, and is not sure that she knows about her place in history—or even that she exists.

The four cases challenging the LRB apportionment plan were consolidated under *Graves v. Barnes* in the Western District, but the panel included Judge William Wayne Justice from the Eastern District along with Judge John H. Wood of the Western District. Richards had gotten Judge Justice on his panel. The Republicans had gotten San Antonio judge John Wood. The third member of the judicial panel was 5th Circuit Court of Appeals Judge Irving Loeb Goldberg.

The LRB's apportionment plan for the Texas House of Representatives utilized countywide multi-member districts encompassing eleven of the twelve most populous counties in the state. Harris County was the exception. Rather than being a countywide district, Harris County was divided into three multi-member districts that corresponded to the boundaries of the three congressional districts located in the county. Why was Harris County an exception to the county-wide districts in the other urban counties? One theory was that if all Harris County districts were decided at-large (countywide), Republicans might win all of them. Dividing the county into those carefully drawn multi-member districts ensured Republicans of winning some seats, but the Democrats would win others and a majority of the county's seats. Classic gerrymandering.

Using multi-member districts may have been a convenient means for the legislature or LRB to avoid the tough political decisions necessary to draw individual districts within the counties, but multi-member districts also operated to submerge political, ethnic, and racial minorities within a larger majority of non-Hispanic white Democrats in each county. Claims of invidious discrimination had been raised against multi-member districts before in Texas in 1960s litigation and already in the '70s in the lawsuit challenging the senate that was filed on behalf of African American legislator Curtis Graves from Dallas. In each of these prior cases, however, the claim was largely secondary, was supported by little or no evidence, and was denied by the courts. This circumstance was about to change.

The district court in *Graves v. Barnes* proceeded to trial. The state asserted that the LRB apportionment plan for the House of Representatives had an acceptable statewide deviation of 9.9 percent. This assertion was contested by the plaintiffs on the basis that the multi-member districts made the true deviation closer to 29.3 percent. The three-judge court found the 9.9 percent excessive. The state had failed to establish any rational or consistent policy that justified the deviation. The court declared the statewide plan in violation of the Fourteenth Amendment but withheld injunctive relief pending appeal to the Supreme Court. The 1972 elections went forward using the single- and multi-member districts in the LRB plan, Dallas and Bexar Counties excepted.

The state pointed out that Texas had often used multi-member electoral districts in the past, but the three-judge court found that the state had failed at trial to provide any rational justification for the "haphazard combination of single- and multi-member districts." The court confined evidence of the unconstitutionality of multi-member districts to those only in Dallas and Bexar counties because under the "inherent time limitations incident to these actions, [the plaintiffs] would have difficulty in fully developing the evidence . . . other than in Dallas and Bexar." The court retained jurisdiction of the claims against the remaining nine counties.

After a full and carefully organized analysis of the evidence offered on Dallas and Bexar Counties, the court found that the multi-member districts in both counties invidiously diluted or cancelled out the vote of racial or ethnic minorities. In Dallas County, the finding pertained to the African American community. In Bexar County, the finding applied to the Latinx community. The court enjoined use of the multi-member districts in these two counties and adopted plans drawing single-member districts in each of these counties to be used in the 1972 elections. The plans were ones submitted by the plaintiffs in the case. Efforts by the state to stay this order failed.

The district court's analysis of the claim of vote dilution against the multi-member districts in Dallas and Bexar Counties, after it was affirmed by the Supreme Court, became and remains the road map for challenging multi-member and at-large districts, and even some single-member districts, nationwide. The latter half of the 1970s and early 1980s saw successful lawsuits challenging the use of multi-member district elections in most of the large cities and school districts in Texas. Subsequent federal court decisions have somewhat altered this road map, but the effect of the district court's decision remains potent today. It also is an example of how an attorney's thoroughly reasoned cause of action and carefully prepared evidentiary showing (not to mention his successful forum shopping) can affect the outcome of not only a single case but also the law nationwide.

The challenge by Republicans to the senatorial districts in Bexar County and the challenge by Curtis Graves to the senatorial districts in Harris County were denied by the district court. The court upheld the constitutionality of the LRB's senatorial districts. The United States Supreme Court affirmed this ruling (*Archer v. Smith*).

WHITE V. REGESTER[2]

The appeal of the *Graves v. Barnes* decision on the House districts led to the momentous Supreme Court decision in *White v. Regester*. In it, the Supreme Court established two significant

---

2. When multiple lawsuits are consolidated, the cases are sometimes reported under different case names in different courts. In this instance, the case known as Graves v. Barnes in the three-judge district court became White v. Regester on appeal at the Supreme Court.

standards that have affected judicial and legislative action for the past forty-seven years.

The court overturned the district court's finding that a showing of a statewide maximum deviation of 9.9 percent among state legislative districts, as opposed to congressional districts, was sufficient to establish that a state's plan was unconstitutional. This ruling led to the so-called "10 percent rule" under which a state legislative apportionment of 9.9 percent or less among districts is presumed valid against a challenge of population inequality. State legislatures have relied on this benchmark for more than four decades. Later cases have shown that this presumption of validity is rebuttable, but the burden of showing invidious discrimination by an apportionment plan with a deviation of less than 10 percent falls on the plaintiffs. States are not automatically required to justify such deviations with acceptable state policy.

The Supreme Court upheld the district court's finding that the use of multi-member legislative districts in Dallas and Bexar Counties was in violation of the Fourteenth Amendment because they were being used invidiously to cancel out or minimize the voting strength of racial minorities. The court concluded that the plaintiffs had produced "evidence to support findings that the political processes leading to nomination and election were not equally open to participation by the group in question in that its members had less opportunity than did other residents in the district to participate in the political processes and to elect legislators of their choice."

Specifically, the court followed the evidentiary road map laid out by the plaintiffs and accepted by the district court, including: the history of invidious discrimination in Texas against these minority groups; the limited success of minority candidates in the past in these specific counties under a multi-member system; the existence of a "slating" system (in which a group of candidates run in multi-seat or multi-position elections on a common platform—in this case, Dallas) dominated by the non-Hispanic white majority that effectively determined who won election under the multi-member structure; consistent reliance on "racial campaign tactics" to defeat "candidates with the overwhelming support" of the minority community; the unresponsiveness of white elected officials to the interests of the minority community; and, implicit in 1973, but later explicitly made a required finding, the presence of polarized voting by a white majority against candidates favored by minority voters.

The court stressed the need in the future for an "intensely local appraisal" of any claims, just as had happened in the Texas case. The court's test of unconstitutionality had an effect nationwide. It also proved controversial, however, particularly insofar as it seemed to some critics to focus on "effects" rather than on "intent." This controversy and subsequent Supreme Court cases finding "intent" to discriminate to be a necessary part of showing invidious discrimination eventually led Congress to amend Section 2 of the Voting Rights Act to incorporate a "results" test. This change will be discussed later.

LATER PROCEEDINGS IN *GRAVES V. BARNES*

In an opinion issued in January 1974, the district court in *Graves* turned its attention to the other nine multi-member districts in the LRB apportionment plan for the Texas House of Representatives. The court found that, using the test of invidious discrimination approved in *Regester*, eight of the nine remaining countywide multi-member districts were unconstitutional. The court found no evidence to support a finding that the multi-member district in Hidalgo County violated the constitution. The court's order requiring eight of the counties to be divided into single-member districts was stayed by the Supreme Court. As a result, the 1974 elections were again carried out using the LRB statewide plan, except for the single-member districts drawn in 1972 for Dallas and Bexar Counties, as the case was appealed.

Fearful of losing this time at the Supreme Court, David Richards and the other plaintiff lawyers turned their attention to having the Texas Legislature draw single-member districts in each of the nine counties in response to this latest holding by the district court. The legislature did so during its regular session in 1975. Advised of the legislature's action, the Supreme Court vacated the district court judgment and remanded the case for reconsideration in light of the legislature's action. Richards later found a copy of the court's draft opinion (never issued) and saw that, as he suspected, the state was going to win in some counties. By this time, however, a new element had been added to the redistricting process. In 1975, Texas was made subject to Section 5 of the Voting Rights Act of 1965.

SECTIONS 4 AND 5 OF THE VOTING RIGHTS ACT

When enacted in 1965, Section 5 of the Voting Rights Act applied to only a select few states and other jurisdictions. Section 4 of the act provided a formula for determining which jurisdictions were "covered" based on whether they had significant African American population, low African American voter turnout, and a "test or device" that infringed on the African Americans' right to vote. If a jurisdiction were subject to Section 5, it could not change any voting qualification or practice without first obtaining a ruling from a DC district court or the attorney general of the United States that the change had neither the purpose nor the effect of denying or abridging the right to vote. This requirement came to be known as "preclearance." Once subject to the formula and the preclearance requirement, a state could virtually never escape. Some smaller jurisdictions were successful in "bailing out" of the preclearance requirement, but no state was successful because of the very rigid requirements for doing so. (These crucial provisions are listed in the appendix.)

Texas was not within the scope of Section 5 of the Voting Rights Act when it was first passed in 1965 because the state did not have a literacy test that impaired African Americans' voting. Some cynical observers point out that it did not hurt that a Texan was in the White House in 1965. In 1975, however, the act's coverage was expanded to include members of a "language minority," and the act's definition of a "test or device" that impaired voting was expanded to include the provision of election materials "only in the English language." This formula was contained in Section 4 of the act.

Texas now had to submit the newly drawn nine single-member district plans for preclearance. Shortly before the 1976 primaries, the attorney general of the United States objected to the new districts in Tarrant, Nueces, and Jefferson Counties. The legislatively enacted districts in these counties could not take effect. The court in *Graves v. Barnes* (III) accepted agreed-upon plans for the court to order in Nueces and Jefferson Counties, but no agreement was reached on a plan for districts in Tarrant County. The state presented evidence that the plaintiffs' proposed plan for that county could not be implemented in time for the impending primary. As a result, the district court adopted as an "interim plan" a state proposal that election officials testified could be implemented in time for the primaries. A year later, the district court substituted the plaintiffs' plan for the interim plan (*Graves v. Barnes* [IV]).

CONGRESSIONAL DISTRICTS

Texas was apportioned an additional seat in Congress in 1971, bringing the number of the state's representatives to twenty-four. The Texas Legislature in special session (June 1971) successfully redrew these twenty-four districts statewide in a plan (designated SB 1) in which the maximum deviation in population from the ideal was only +2.43 percent and –1.7 percent (a total maximum deviation of 4.13 percent). Nevertheless, although this degree of disparity was far smaller than for the state's congressional plans in the 1960s, it was not sufficient to avoid a finding by the federal district court that the plan violated the Fourteenth Amendment. The population deviations were not "unavoidable."

For a remedy, the district court was presented with several alternative plans for use in the forthcoming 1972 elections. One (labeled Plan B) largely adhered to the district lines in the state enactment but with a lower population deviation (.149 percent). Another (labeled Plan C) made no effort to adhere to the district lines in the state enactment. The total maximum deviation in Plan C was .284 percent. The district court chose Plan C as its remediation plan, largely because it considered this plan to be "significantly more compact and contiguous" and to "best effectuate the principle of 'one man, one vote'" because it was drawn solely on the basis of population without consideration of the political decisions reflected in the original legislative enactment.

The United States Supreme Court (*White v. Weiser*) affirmed the district court's finding that the deviation in the legislative enactment was too great and that SB 1 was unconstitutional. In a decision that has often been misconstrued, the court reversed the district court's adoption of Plan C. The court did not explicitly make its decision based on the lower deviation in Plan B. Instead, the court found that in choosing between two acceptable remedial apportionment plans, a district court should defer to state policy so long as the result redresses any constitutional violations. The state policy in question was the preservation to the extent possible of the constituencies of congressional incumbents—"preserving member-constituent relations."

The court reiterated that a policy of minimizing the number of contests between incumbents does not in and of itself establish invidiousness. It is important in applying *Weiser* to realize that the court was not speaking of the legitimacy of a state policy of drawing districts to be more Democratic or Republican or to benefit incumbents with "safe" districts but of retaining existing district boundaries as best as possible as a means of preserving member-constituent relations and seniority in Congress. The ostensible "interest" being served was a public interest, not the self-interest of the incumbent. It is incorrect to claim that *Weiser* stands for the broad proposition that "incumbent protection" is a legitimate state policy that justifies population deviation.

THE CONSTITUTIONAL CONVENTION OF 1974

In January 1974, pursuant to a constitutional amendment approved by voters two years earlier, the legislature assembled as a constitutional convention. A special Constitutional Revision Commission had been appointed in 1973 to conduct hearings and to recommend constitutional changes to the convention. It was my privilege to serve as a counsel for the commission and the convention. State senators and representatives were equal delegates. The Speaker of the House, Price Daniel, was the presiding officer.

After seven months of haggling, the convention adjourned, having fallen three votes short of the two-thirds vote needed for adoption of the new constitution. The final sticking point was whether the proposed constitution should include a provision on right-to-work. The state's labor unions strongly opposed such a provision, while many of the state's businesses and most Republican legislators strongly favored it. During the legislative session that occurred the following year, Lieutenant Governor Bill Hobby was able to resurrect the final document and win approval to submit it for a statewide vote. The state's voters rejected the constitutional rewrite.

EFFECTS

The effects in Texas of the *Graves* and *Regester* decisions were substantial. The elimination of multi-member districts in the urban counties as a means of gerrymandering brought immediate changes in the makeup of the legislative delegations from those counties.

Moreover, it now was clear that the Texas Legislature could no longer gerrymander by doing nothing when the federal decennial census showed the state's congressional or legislative districts to be unequal in population. *Graves v. Barnes* showed that the federal courts could not only declare state redistricting enactments invalid but also adopt remedial plans instead of leaving it to the legislature to do so. Usually, these court-ordered plans were ones submitted by the plaintiff groups and were unfriendly to the incumbents who had gerrymandered the overturned plan.

By the end of the decade, there were fourteen African Americans and seventeen Hispanics in the Texas House of Representatives. All the African Americans came from the state's urban areas, including Jefferson County. Republicans, too, benefited from the recent court decisions. The number of Republicans in the Texas House of Representatives climbed from ten in 1971 to thirty-five by 1981. The dominance of the non-Hispanic white Democrats in the state legislature was waning.

In Congress, the changes came more slowly. Probably because the *Weiser* decision resulted in use of a congressional plan designed to maintain "member-constituent relations," which at the time meant districts that had elected twenty Democrats and four Republicans, Republicans gained only a single additional congressional seat during the decade despite statewide voting strength of approximately 45 percent in congressional elections. With Barbara Jordan's election from

Harris County, the first African American joined the state congressional delegation but at the cost of the only African American state senator. Hispanics too increased their representation in Congress, but only slowly over the decade.

Of importance during this period was the "shocking" victory of Republican Bill Clements in the race for governor in 1978. He was the first Republican elected to that office since Edmund J. Davis in 1869. Also of note was that Texas's subjection to the preclearance requirement of the Voting Rights Act would prove integral to the state's redistricting for the next four decades.

CHAPTER 6

POLITICAL SEA CHANGE IN TEXAS (1981–2000)

TEXAS DOES NOT ASK a person's political leanings or affiliation when the person registers to vote. Thus, there is no official record of whether a person is likely to vote for Republicans, Democrats, or another party's candidates. As a result, race and ethnicity have increasingly become proxies for partisan affiliation in redistricting. An overwhelming majority of African American (85 to 90 percent) and a significant majority of Hispanic (>65 percent) voters in Texas have voted consistently for Democratic candidates in this century. Conversely, a majority of Anglo voters have consistently voted for Republican candidates.

The first story of gerrymandering in Texas is of Anglo-Democrat dominance and political stagnation. As the twentieth century crept towards its conclusion, however, things began to change. Courts engendered precedents that created more avenues for lawsuits about redistricting. All the while, Texas was urbanizing and diversifying, complicating its apportionment and the practice of equalizing representation.

In 1981, the Texas Legislature passed bills reapportioning the Texas House of Representatives, the Texas Senate, and the state's twenty-seven congressional districts. Unlike in prior decades, however, the plans could become effective only when and if they were precleared under the Voting Rights Act. This circumstance created avenues for increased minority representation. All the while, one wing of the Democratic Party was morphing into the core of the Republican Party, foreshadowing a new chapter in the political story of Texas. All these storylines came crashing together in the final decades of the twentieth century.

STATE LEGISLATIVE DISTRICTS

After the 1981 reapportionment, in rapid succession, the state legislative plans succumbed even before reaching the Department of Justice for review. Republican governor Bill Clements vetoed the senate plan, thereby sending the issue of senate reapportionment once again to the Legislative Redistricting Board. Many wondered about the wisdom of Clements' action since, in 1981, the five statewide officials composing the board were all Democrats.

As in the 1970s, the plan apportioning the House of Representatives was challenged in state court for cutting counties in violation of Article III, Section 26, of the Texas Constitution. Many people (including myself) were shocked that the House plan cut thirty-four county boundaries—a clear mistake in the face of the Texas Supreme Court's ruling a decade earlier in *Smith v. Craddick* in which the apportionment plan cut thirty-three counties. The House committee on redistricting apparently was convinced to disregard the advice of expert witnesses in favor of the mistaken thinking of legislator-lawyers on the committee. This time, the attack in state court came from a Democratic member of the state legislature, Robert Valles, but the outcome was the same.

The legislative enactment was found to violate the Texas Constitution and was declared invalid in its entirety (*Valles v. Clements*).

This case was the worst professional experience of my life. I had been retained in 1980 by the senate through the Legislative Council to prepare a legal guide for redistricting. In my written report and oral testimony, I repeatedly warned the House Committee on Redistricting against cutting county lines unless necessary to comply with federal law. I learned much later that Vice Chairman of the House Committee Bob Davis persuaded his colleagues on the committee to disregard my warning because he believed the Texas Supreme Court would defer to the legislature. This clearly was erroneous advice. I was unaware of what the House Committee was doing.

When I saw the plan for the first time after passage, I was as surprised as anyone. I told the House Committee counsel that the cuts were a problem, but she assured me that the committee had objective, verifiable justification for each cut. I should have demanded to see the justification, but I was so angry at the committee's disregard of my legal advice that I avoided the committee chair, Democrat Tim Von Dohlen. Later, I was retained to aid the attorney general's office in defense of the plan.

At trial, Von Dohlen testified glowingly (probably too much so) at length about my research, written report, and testimony, but without mentioning my warning about cutting county boundaries. He then gave the same justification for each of the cuts: that they were made "on advice of legal counsel." He never named me as the attorney who gave such advice, which would have been a lie, but everyone in the courtroom (except Von Dohlen and me), including the judge, assumed that he was referring to me. What should I have done? I could not object to my client's testimony without damaging his case, so I remained silent. The district court ruled against the state.

On appeal, I defended the committee's actions as best I could. I lost. This is my first public comment on what happened.

THE LEGISLATIVE REDISTRICTING BOARD IN 1982

As a result of these events, the state's job of apportioning state legislative districts once again came to rest with the LRB. The board consisted of all Democrats, but a division on the board was evident.

Lieutenant Governor Bill Hobby and Speaker of the House of Representatives Bill Clayton were aligned to support redistricting plans that generally protected the incumbent members of their respective chambers of the legislature. However, tension grew between Clayton and Bob Armstrong, the Commissioner of the General Land Office, who proposed amendments to House districts in Harris, Dallas, and Bexar Counties. Armstrong's amendments were supported by racial and ethnic minority interests and were adopted when Armstrong garnered the votes of Comptroller Bob Bullock and Attorney General Mark White.

Another political undercurrent played out on the board. All but Speaker Clayton had his eyes on becoming governor. Thus, each action taken by a member of the board had potential ramifications for that individual's chances to win the Democratic nomination. Lt. Governor Hobby had worked with Governor Clements during the legislative sessions and was not inclined to run against his reelection. Bullock disliked Hobby and so generally opposed any Hobby proposal on the board. He refrained from seeking the Democratic nomination for governor in 1982 but became lieutenant governor in 1990. Both Bob Armstrong and Mark White sought the Democratic nomination for governor in 1982. White won the primary and defeated the reelection bid of the Republican candidate, Bill Clements, in the general election.

By a 4–1 vote on October 27 and 28, the LRB adopted apportionment plans for the Texas Senate and House of Representatives. Comptroller Bob Bullock dissented on the adoption of both chambers' plans.

STATE LITIGATION

A lawsuit filed by Republicans in state court challenged the LRB plan because the latter drew senate districts using population instead of "qualified electors" as specified at the time in Article III, Section 25, of the Texas Constitution (*Upham v. White*). Section 25 had been ruled unconstitutional during the 1960s, but the argument in 1981 was that this ruling applied only to the section's requirement that no county have more than one senator. A state district court ruled against the Republican challenge. The Texas Supreme Court on appeal ultimately dismissed the case without ruling on the status of Section 25 or the legality of using population instead of qualified electors. Section 25 was later amended to delete the reference to qualified electors.

FEDERAL LITIGATION

The predictable federal court challenges quickly followed. A challenge of the senate apportionment plan was filed in the Northern District of Texas by a largely Republican group of plaintiffs ("senate plaintiffs"). A second case challenging the House of Representative districts was filed in the Western District of Texas ("House plaintiffs"). A third case was filed in the Western District by the mayor and City of Baytown claiming that the LRB house plan impermissibly divided communities and units of interest (e.g., Baytown) with the intent of underrepresenting these areas. These cases were consolidated in the Northern District, with two district judges from that district, Judge Barefoot Sanders and Judge Jerry Buchmeyer, and one justice from the 5th Circuit Court of Appeals, Judge Carolyn Dineen Randall. Intervenors included Montgomery County and Hispanic citizens represented by MALDEF, which played a major role in the case.

The state's submission of the LRB apportionment plans to the DOJ for review under Section 5 of the Voting Rights Act took an unusual turn. The Democratic Texas attorney general made a submission on November 23 urging preclearance of the LRB plans. One week later, the Republican Texas secretary of state made his own submission, noting in his submission letter, "It has come to my attention that the submitted Plan may not comply with the Voting Rights Act in all respects." Allegations of Section 5 violations were attached to the letter. The Department of Justice accepted the secretary of state's submission as the state's official submission.

While the redistricting plans were pending before the Department of Justice, a six-day trial commenced in federal court on January 18, 1982. The DOJ declined to attend. Two days after the trial concluded, the Department of Justice issued an objection under Section 5 to specific parts of the House and senate plans. The members of the court were furious at the DOJ's timing. The DOJ indicated that "the state has failed to demonstrate that the plan is [racially and ethnically] nondiscriminatory." This finding was understandable in view of the position of the secretary of state in his submission letter but was not fully understandable to the court in view of the testimony that it had just heard. Nevertheless, the DOJ objections meant that the LRB plans were legally unenforceable and could not be used for the rapidly approaching May 1 primary elections. The DOJ subsequently modified its objections, but the LRB plans remained legally unenforceable.

The court faced a dilemma. It had heard six days of testimony on the constitutional and statutory claims against the LRB plans, but the failure of the plans to obtain preclearance under Section 5 of the Voting Rights Act foreclosed the court from ruling on these claims. All the parties to the litigation asked the court to adopt interim or permanent plans to be used for the upcoming elections. The court agreed to do so, noting that "[o]ur task is to devise a remedy but without having adjudicated a violation on which to predicate that remedy." Given the constraints of time, the court indicated that it would devise an interim plan by beginning with the LRB apportionment plans and making "only such modifications to those plans as would be necessary."

Many of the parties submitted redrawn apportionment plans for the parts of the state subject to the DOJ objections. House Speaker Clayton also presented alternatives. After considering the various proposals, the court adopted the following changes to the LRB plan for House of Representatives districts: in Bexar County, the MALDEF proposal was adopted over those submitted by the House plaintiffs and Speaker Clayton; in El Paso County, the MALDEF proposal was adopted over one from Speaker Clayton; in Dallas County, the LRB's original plan was considered superior to those offered by MALDEF, the House plaintiffs, and Speaker Clayton.

The court also rejected the so-called "de minimis plans" (from MALDEF, the House plaintiffs, and Speaker Clayton) that would have redrawn the entire state with a much lower population deviation than in the LRB plan. The court found that adoption of the LRB House plan—except in Bexar, Dallas, and El Paso—as the court's interim plan was justified by the "exigencies of the situation," such as the avoidance of a disruption of the state's electoral process, even though the resulting statewide deviation (9.95 percent) of the plan was higher than in these alternative statewide plans. The court also noted that the higher deviation of the LRB plan was caused in large part by the decision to keep Gregg County intact and that some of the alternative de minimis statewide plans split many more counties than the LRB plan, in possible violation of the Texas Constitution.

For the Texas Senate, the court considered and rejected alternative proposals for Harris County and Bexar County. Ultimately, the court adopted the entire LRB senate plan for use as an interim plan. Appeals to the US Supreme Court were unsuccessful, and the district court's interim plans were used for the 1982 elections.

In 1983, the focus turned to whether the court's interim plans should become permanent. The legislature in 1983 elected to leave the court plan in effect rather than pass legislation that either adopted the court plan or changed it. There was one exception. Minor modifications were approved by the legislature for the court's senatorial districts in Harris and Bexar Counties to address the DOJ objections and MALDEF concerns. The Texas Legislature feared that enacting a new senate reapportionment bill might negate the senators' staggered terms, causing them to have to run for election again in 1984. To avoid this possible outcome, the legislature passed a concurrent resolution containing these modifications rather than a bill.

These modifications were submitted to the district court with the agreement of MALDEF and adopted by the court as part of its permanent senate plan. Agreement could not be reached, however, on the House of Representatives districts in Dallas County. The dispute was basically between the county's Hispanic and African American communities about how the predominantly minority districts should be drawn. After an evidentiary hearing, the court rejected MALDEF's challenge. For the remainder of the decade, members of the Texas House of Representatives and senate were elected from the districts in the modified court plans (*Terrazas v. Clements*).

CONGRESSIONAL DISTRICTS

In 1981, Texas's number of seats in Congress increased from twenty-four to twenty-seven. The congressional apportionment plan adopted by the legislature, however, was vetoed by Governor Bill Clements. Three special sessions followed.

The dispute between the Republican governor and the Democrat-controlled legislature was over Clements' demand that the congressional plan contain a predominantly minority congressional district in Dallas County. The creation of such a district required consolidating most of the African American and Hispanic population from the other nearby districts, thereby removing many of the dependably Democratic voters from those districts and leaving the districts likely to elect a Republican instead of reelecting the incumbent Democrats. Democrats opposed such a result. The Democratic incumbent most at risk appeared to be Jim Mattox (District 5). The standoff dragged on into the summer. Finally, the legislature in special session passed an apportionment plan that contained a majority-minority district in Dallas County that satisfied Clements. The legislature did not ultimately succumb to Clements but instead changed its position because of African American testimony during the special sessions in favor of creating this district.

Litigation challenging the congressional plan was filed in the Eastern District of Texas. District judges William Wayne Justice, who had served on the panel in the *Graves* case, and Robert Parker were appointed to the court, along with Judge Sam Johnson of the 5th Circuit Court of Appeals. The court held an evidentiary hearing but withheld any ruling while waiting for the DOJ decision under Section 5 of the Voting Rights Act. On January 29, 1982, the DOJ acted.

The letter from the attorney general of the United States indicated that the state "has satisfied its burden of

demonstrating that the submitted plan is nondiscriminatory in purpose and effect" except for Districts 15 and 27 in
South Texas. The court's plan for this area divided the heavily Hispanic population in Hidalgo and Cameron counties
and joined these counties in two districts with less-Hispanic
counties to the north to avoid packing Hispanics in a single
compact district. These elongated districts, due to their shape,
have been referred to as "bacon-strip districts." This same
basic configuration still may be found in current congressional redistricting plans. Critically, the DOJ did not object to
the districts drawn by the legislature in Dallas. The objection
letter made the state's congressional plan legally unenforceable, so the court adopted an interim plan that redrew the
two districts to meet the DOJ objection.

In addition, however, a majority of the court decided to
redraw the districts in Dallas County (Districts 5, 24, 3, and
26) to once again divide the county's minority communities
among several districts, particularly 5 and 24, with the effect
of restoring the Democratic majorities (*Seamon v. Upham*).
The court reasoned that the Democratic incumbents in those
districts had been responsive to minority interests in the
past, that the new majority-minority district was not necessarily a "safe" minority seat, and that the creation of one possibly minority district in lieu of two districts with responsive
congressmen was potentially retrogressive in the context of a
federal court plan. Judge Robert Parker dissented. Republican
officials requested a stay and an expedited appeal. The state
also appealed.

I appeared many times in cases before Chief District Judge
Justice, one of the three judges charged with redrawing the
congressional districting plan in light of the DOJ objection,
both as an assistant attorney general and later in private
practice. In my opinion, he was an outstanding judge who
had a significant positive effect on Texas, particularly when it
comes to prisons, education, and redistricting. This was the

only time I felt that his decision was purely political. No one could have sat through the extensive legislative hearings on the Dallas districts and not felt that African American voters wanted the predominantly African American district.

The Supreme Court denied the stay but expedited the appeal. On April 1, 1982, the court (*Upham v. Seamon*) reversed the district court's decision regarding the congressional districts in Dallas County. Relying on its 1972 decision in *Weiser*, the court held that, even though the DOJ objection made the state enactment unenforceable statewide, the three-judge court was not free to modify the state's plan other than in the area subject to the DOJ objection in the absence of a finding of a constitutional or statutory violation.

The court also recognized, however, that the state was asking that any remedy be delayed until 1983 because it would be too disruptive to revert to the original apportionment plan in Dallas given the proximity of the primary elections. On remand, a majority of the district court retained its redrawn apportionment plan for Dallas County for the upcoming 1982 elections. These districts, plus those in South Texas and a few modifications statewide, were then codified by the legislature in 1983 without fear of a gubernatorial veto, since Republican Bill Clements had been defeated for reelection in 1982.

THORNBURG V. GINGLES

The most important redistricting decision in the 1980s was *Thornburg v. Gingles* (1986). Congress in 1982 had amended Section 2 of the Voting Rights Act to provide a meaningful right of redress for racial and ethnic minorities nationwide by allowing a violation to be shown by effect alone, rather than by a showing of discriminatory intent. This impermissible "result" of the actions of a state or political subdivision was to be shown by the "totality of circumstances." This test was essentially the same one, with consideration of many of the same factors, as used in *Graves* and *Regester*.

In *Gingles*, the court, in an opinion delivered by Justice William Brennan, agreed that the totality of factors listed by Congress was relevant to a claim of vote dilution due to the submergence of minority voters in an at-large district but concluded that such factors are insufficient to show a violation of Section 2 unless the following circumstances exist: Minority voters must constitute a geographically insular community that is large enough to be a majority in a fair single-member district; there must be a bloc-voting Anglo majority that usually defeats candidates supported by a racial minority; and the minority voters must be politically cohesive.

In a complicated set of mixed concurrences and partial dissents, the members of the court expressed differing views about what constituted legally sufficient bloc voting and the importance of prior success by minority candidates. The requirements from *Gingles* remain a significant part of any vote dilution case, at-large or single member.

CONSEQUENCES

The LRB senate plan, which remained virtually unchanged by the court in *Terrazas*, purposefully drew a district in Harris County in which African American voters could elect the person of their choice. Former state representative African American Craig Washington was thus elected to the Texas Senate in 1982. A strongly African American senate district was also drawn in Dallas County, but incumbent white Democrat Oscar Mauzy continued to be elected.

In the Texas House of Representatives, there continued to be fourteen African American representatives, all Democrats elected from heavily African American districts in urban areas. These districts had their origin in the single-member districts drawn in *Graves*. Preservation of these heavily

African American districts, subject to the requirement for population equality, was legally necessary in 1981 because Section 5 of the Voting Rights Act prevented any "retrogression" of minority voting rights. Section 5 also prevented any retrogression in Hispanic voting strength, while the increase in Hispanic population necessarily resulted in an increase in the number of Hispanic state representatives (17 to 20) and senators (4 to 5).

Bill Clements' reelection loss in 1982 marked a steep drop in the Republican vote statewide to 40 percent. The Republican vote recovered, however, and by 1991 the number of Republican congressmen had grown to eight, including Tom DeLay, who was first elected in 1984. In the state legislature, fifty-seven of the 150 members of the House of Representatives and eight of the thirty-one members of the senate were Republican by 1991.

Meanwhile, another phenomenon was occurring. As more and more people began to vote for Republicans and as racial and ethnic minorities and liberals became more prevalent in the Democratic Party, members of the conservative wing of that party began to abandon it and become Republican. John Tower was initially a Democrat but switched to being a Republican before his election as US senator. John Connally, a Democratic governor of Texas, switched to the Republican Party in 1973. Phil Gramm switched from Democrat to Republican in 1983 and was elected US senator from Texas in 1985.

The phenomenon of politicians switching parties occurred across the South as Republican voting strength grew. It reached its peak in Texas in the 1980s, when future leaders of the Republican Party, such as Rick Perry, Tom DeLay, and Kent Hance, switched from the Democratic Party. Demonstrably, the conservative wing of the Democratic Party essentially morphed into the core of the Republican Party.

A DEMOCRATIC STRATEGY FAILS

In 1991, the Democrats still controlled both chambers of the Texas Legislature. The governor, Ann Richards, and the attorney general, Dan Morales, also were Democrats. The legislature set out to draw this state's congressional, state senate, and House districts in a manner that would enhance African American and Hispanic voting strength but also reelect incumbents, especially Democratic incumbents.

Democratic leaders were caught in a three-sided vise. The state's rural areas were clearly Republican, as judged by voting in state and federal statewide races. These areas could not be sliced in any way to produce a Democratic stronghold or even a Democratic majority according to data from these races. The Democrats' only hope in the rural areas was that the few Democratic incumbents could hang on by continuing to win the vote of their constituents willing to split their vote between Republican and Democrat. Federal precedent, *Weiser v. White*, favored a minimal change in these districts. A second side of the vise was provided by the incumbents, both Democratic and Republican, who expected redistricting plans that protected them. Any plan ignoring the plight of incumbents was unlikely to receive the votes necessary for adoption.

The remaining side of the vise was provided by minorities and Section 5 of the Voting Rights Act. The votes of African Americans and Hispanics were becoming increasingly important to the Democratic Party, but the days of gathering these minority votes for non-Hispanic white candidates was largely gone. For almost two decades, the redistricting plans crafted by the Democrat-controlled legislature had been struck down by the DOJ under Section 5 of the Voting Rights Act. The argument by Hispanic activist organizations, such as MALDEF, in 1991 was strengthened by the fact that the fastest growing census cohort and some of the fastest growing counties in the 1980s were primarily Hispanic. Redistricting plans that clearly enhanced minority voting strength were expected to win DOJ preclearance and thus leave the plans legally enforceable and avoid court intervention.

A problem in this approach was how to craft districts that were likely to elect racial and ethnic minorities and still retain districts that were likely to reelect incumbent non-Hispanic white Democrats. This strategy was made easier for the congressional districts because the state had three newly apportioned seats. All three seats were drawn so that they favored the election of Hispanic or African American candidates. However, it was much harder for the state legislative district plans because there were no additional seats to be allocated, but the interests of incumbents were to be considered. As a result, while minority activist groups were satisfied with the congressional plan, they viewed the state legislative plans as inadequate. Republicans opposed all the state's redistricting plans in part because an increase in minority districts meant a probable increase in Democratic seats. Republicans blamed Democratic congressman Martin Frost for gerrymandering the 1991 congressional districts to prevent increasing the number of Republican congressmen.

The method selected by the legislature for trying to achieve its goals was to use the smallest available census geography, census blocks, to parse minority population, as a proxy for Democratic voters, among districts in the urban areas. This was a mistake that led to districts that were bizarre in appearance while ultimately achieving little, if any, increase in minority representation than was possible with more compact and regularly shaped districts. Plans redrawing all congressional and state legislative districts were successfully enacted by the legislature and submitted to the DOJ for preclearance. Despite, or in some cases because of, the

legislature's effort to draw districts enhancing minority voting strength, however, lawsuits still followed.

LIBERAL DEMOCRATIC AND MINORITY
LITIGATION STRATEGY

It is appropriate at this point to remind readers that although
a sizeable majority of Hispanic and African American voters
supported Democratic candidates, minority activist organizations, especially Hispanic ones, took pride in not doing so.
They claimed to be apolitical and interested only in enhancing the voting strength of their respective racial or ethnic
group. Democratic leaders could control what the legislature enacted, but the party's lawyers knew that the Hispanic
activist organizations and Republicans would challenge the
enactments in court.

Liberal Democrats and Hispanic organizations realized
that the outcome of such litigation in federal court was uncertain, especially now that Judge Justice had taken senior judge
status and might not be part of any three-judge panel hearing
the case. Guided by David Richards, they envisioned the possibility of litigation in which lawyers for the state, Hispanic
activist groups such as MALDEF, and the DOJ could come
up with agreed redistricting plans for the senate and House
that all could live with and that did not cater to the wishes of
incumbents.

There were two key factors for favorable litigation. The
attorney general (representing the state) was Democrat Dan
Morales, who could be expected to cooperate, but there was no
guarantee that a federal court would go along. However, state
district judges were elected locally. Thus, a state court in an
area preferably Hispanic that consistently voted Democratic
might be a friendly forum.

CENSUS LITIGATION

The first case (*Mena v. Richards*) was filed by Hispanic plaintiffs in state court on February 7, 1991, in heavily Hispanic Hidalgo County in South Texas before the legislature even had a full opportunity to redistrict. This lawsuit alleged that the federal decennial census undercounted Mexican Americans and African Americans in Texas and asked that the census numbers be adjusted in redistricting to offset this undercount. A similar federal lawsuit was filed shortly thereafter in the Southern District of Texas. This latter lawsuit in federal court never proceeded.

The state litigation (*Mena v. Richards*) went forward with a hearing on August 5, 1991. The state court declared that the federal decennial census undercounted minority populations in Texas and ordered the state to come up with new reapportionment plans using adjusted numbers. The state appealed. Even though Attorney General Dan Morales was generally sympathetic with the goals of the Hispanic plaintiffs, the state was fearful that drawing apportionment plans with adjusted census numbers pursuant to a state court order would leave such plans in violation of the United States Constitution. The Texas Supreme Court stayed the order in *Mena*. Despite this pending litigation, the state's redistricting plans used the census enumerations without officially adjusting them for any alleged undercount.

These suits were later amended to challenge the state's redistricting plans after they were enacted. Therefore, even though the litigation to alter the census numbers had been unsuccessful, the Democrats had a state court forum in which to develop friendly redistricting plans.

THE STATE SENATE

Nineteen of thirty-one state senators, mostly the Democrats, reached an agreement on October 7 with the *Mena* plaintiffs for a redrawing of senatorial districts. Since the *Mena* litigation was still stayed, a new lawsuit, *Quiroz v. Richards*, was filed in the same court with an agreed judgment on senate district boundaries. After entry of this agreed judgment by the state court, the Democratic Texas secretary of state advised the DOJ that this new agreed plan was being substituted for the legislature's senate apportionment plan then pending preclearance.

This new *Quiroz* plan was precleared under Section 5 of the Voting Rights Act on November 18, 1991. With such preclearance, the plan should have become legally enforceable for the 1992 elections, except that the Republicans, who had not intervened in the *Quiroz* proceedings at the district court, challenged the agreed judgment before the Supreme Court of Texas. This court on December 17, 1991, held that, although the attorney general of Texas has general authority to negotiate settlements (including one such as in *Quiroz*), the trial court had abused its discretion by accepting the agreed plan without any adversary proceeding given the tremendous impact of a plan apportioning state legislative districts (*Terrazas v. Ramirez*). The district court's order was vacated, again leaving the state without a precleared redistricting plan for the senate.

THE HOUSE OF REPRESENTATIVES

The legislation apportioning the Texas House of Representatives did not win preclearance from the DOJ. A settlement was reached between the state and the plaintiffs in *Mena* on a modification to the boundaries of the state House of Representative districts designed to remedy the DOJ objections. The effect of this settlement, however, was effectively nullified given the outcome before the Texas Supreme Court in *Quiroz*. The liberal Democrat and Hispanic activist organization strategy to get state court-ordered plans for the House and senate had failed.

THE CONGRESSIONAL DISTRICTS

The goal of increasing minority representation from Texas in Congress was facilitated by the addition of three new congressional seats in Texas, raising the total to thirty districts. All three of the new seats (Districts 28, 29, and 30) were drawn to favor minority voters. Hispanic and African American candidates won the districts in 1992, and all Republican incumbents were reelected.

Although the legislature's congressional plan protected Republican incumbents, Republicans were furious because they believed that one, or more, of these new congressional seats should have been drawn to favor Republicans given that party's increase in the vote statewide. In 2003, Republicans urged that the "re-redistricting of congressional seats" was in part "payback" for the Democrat-controlled congressional redistricting in 1991.

The state court litigation described in the sections above did not affect the legislature's congressional districts plan because it was not part of the litigation in *Mena* or *Quiroz*. While those state court cases involving the state House and senate plans were proceeding, the legislature's congressional plan received preclearance from the DOJ.

On December 24, 1991, the federal court in *Terrazas v. Slagle* approved the legislature's enactment for use in the 1992 elections. This court ruling somewhat belies the claim that the 1991 congressional plan was primarily a plan designed to hurt Republicans. There probably has been no court in Texas redistricting history more blatantly pro-Republican in its rulings than the court in *Terrazas v. Slagle* under the guidance of Judge Nowlin. If the court had found actionable anti-Republican animus in the congressional plan, it almost certainly would have acted. It did not do so. All Republican incumbents won reelection and one Democrat (Albert Bustamante) was replaced by a Republican.

Also, as discussed later in this chapter, the districts under-
went a redrawing in 1996 by the district court in *Vera v. Bush*
in a case brought by Republicans on the basis that the districts in the urban areas were racial gerrymanders. I realize
that my position is contrary to the view in *The Almanac of
American Politics* (1994) and to the argument made by some
Republicans that the 2003 redistricting was simply payback
for 1991. I believe they are wrong. These districts were used
again in the 1994 elections.

FEDERAL COURT LITIGATION ON THE HOUSE AND SENATE DISTRICTS

On May 23, 1991, Republican plaintiffs filed three lawsuits
in federal court separately challenging the legislative enactments apportioning the congressional, state senate, and state
House of Representatives district plans. The suits alleged that
the plans violated the Voting Rights Act and the Fourteenth
and Fifteenth Amendments. Prominent in the suits was a
claim that each of the plans was a partisan gerrymander.

　　The three lawsuits were consolidated, and a three-judge
panel was convened. While the shenanigans played out in
state court, the federal court watched and waited (*Terrazas v.
Slagle*). On several occasions, the federal court was asked to
intervene in the state process by enjoining all or part of the
state court proceedings, but it declined to do so. On December
10, the court began a four-day hearing. By December 24,
1992, the federal court felt that it was time to act.

　　In previous decades, different federal courts often heard
challenges to the congressional and state legislative districts.
In 1991, however, the three-judge court in *Terrazas v. Slagle*
had jurisdiction over all the state's redistricting enactments.
The court consisted of US District Judges James Nowlin and
Walter Smith and 5th Circuit Court of Appeals Judge Will

Garwood. Democrats were particularly concerned about the presence of Judge Nowlin on this panel because he had previously been a Republican state representative and had played a major role in the 1981 redistricting, including being a witness in federal court on behalf of Republicans challenging the LRB's apportionment plans. Nevertheless, Judge Nowlin remained on the court.

In its "Christmas Eve order," the court in *Terrazas* allowed the congressional apportionment plan to stand as an interim plan for use in 1992 since it had been precleared by the DOJ. It concluded, however, that there was no legally enforceable plan for either the senate or the House of Representatives.

Many different possible redistricting plans, including the agreed plans from *Quiroz* and *Mena*, were submitted to the court for possible implementation in the 1992 elections for the state House and senate. Instead of using one of these plans, a majority of the court fashioned its own interim plans for the senate and House of Representatives and extended the filing deadlines for the primary to January 10, 1992. Judge Nowlin admitted to secretly talking with then-current members of the House and using, or having his staff use, the state's (Texas Legislative Council's) computers to fashion the court's plans for the senate and House. The Democrats, through Attorney General Dan Morales, accused him of bias for Republicans and for his former desk mate from the legislature, who was planning to run for the senate. Nowlin was ultimately publicly reprimanded for his actions by the 5th Circuit Court of Appeals and recused himself from the case, but the plans remained in effect.

Judge Garwood agreed with the majority's decision that court-ordered plans were necessary under the circumstances but, noting that the Texas Legislature had been called into special session for the purpose of redistricting, felt that the court's order should expressly recognize that a valid legislative plan would take precedence over the court's interim plan. The Democrat-controlled Texas Legislature met in a short special session on January 2–8, 1992, and enacted the federal court's interim plan for the House of Representatives as a permanent plan. The legislature, however, rejected the court's senate apportionment plan and, instead, enacted legislation embodying the plan from the *Quiroz* litigation.

A majority of the court in *Terrazas* refused to substitute the legislature's senate plan in lieu of the court's own plan. This majority questioned the motives behind the plan. The majority concluded, "[I]t appears that the Senate was primarily interested in fashioning a plan that better protects certain Anglo incumbents at the expense of minority voters' ability to elect candidates of their choice" and "the Senate has only engaged in time-consuming partisanship." It found that the enacted plan did less to enhance minority voting strength than the court's interim plan, and worried that substitution of the enacted plan for the court plan would "necessarily and needlessly" result in postponement of the 1992 primary elections. Judge Garwood again dissented.

Democrats viewed this ruling of the *Terrazas* court rejecting the legislature's senate districts as partisan. As a result, the State of Texas sought a stay of the federal court order and removal of Judge Nowlin from the panel. The state also filed a declaratory judgment action in the district court for the District of Columbia seeking preclearance of the legislature's new senate plan. The state's primary elections, however, went ahead on March 10, 1992, using the *Terrazas* court's plan for the senate.

The DC court later precleared the legislature's enactment on September 17, 1992, but it was too late to use the plan for the upcoming general election. Democratic Secretary of State John Hannah's direction on August 6, 1992, that the upcoming general elections for the senate must be conducted on the basis of the now precleared legislative enactment, was quickly enjoined by the *Terrazas* court. Thus, the 1992 general elections went forward using the court plan for the senate.

In 1993, the court in *Terrazas* reconvened to consider the Republican plaintiffs' substantive claims of unconstitutionality against the state-enacted apportionment plans. By now, Judge Nowlin was no longer on the panel. His place had been taken by District Judge Harry Hudspeth. The court was now obviously led by Judge Garwood. It rejected all the plaintiffs' claims, including those directed at the senate plan adopted by the legislature in 1992. The court was particularly skeptical of the plaintiffs' claims of partisan gerrymandering. This time, Judge Smith dissented and would have granted summary judgment holding the legislature's senate plan unconstitutional.

The court's approval of the legislative enactments came too late to save the Democrats. The 1992 senate election, which had been held under the court's interim plan, was devastating for Democrats: four incumbent Democratic senators went down in defeat, and no Republican incumbent lost. Altogether, Republicans won thirteen seats in the senate. The now precleared and court-approved legislative plan for the senate was used for the 1994 elections but did little to stop the Democratic slide. With subsequent retirements or losses by Democratic senators, the Republicans soon had a majority of sixteen seats in the senate.

THE DEPARTMENT OF JUSTICE AND RACIAL GERRYMANDERING

Challenges to the legality of the state's apportionment plans did not end with the ruling by the court in *Terrazas*. In 1993, the Supreme Court of the United States held that a plaintiff states a valid constitutional claim by alleging that a state redistricting plan, on its face, has no rational explanation except as an effort to separate voters on the basis of race (*Shaw v. Reno*).

Two years later, the court considered the role that Department of Justice policy under Section 5 of the Voting Rights Act had played in Georgia's choice of congressional redistricting plans (*Miller v. Johnson*). The court found that there was little doubt that Georgia's true motivation in choosing the boundaries of its minority districts was to satisfy Justice Department preclearance demands, not to remedy the effects of past discrimination. The Supreme Court, in an opinion by Justice Anthony Kennedy, criticized the DOJ for what the court called its "maximization" policy for minorities. He reasoned that just because the DOJ required such a policy for preclearance did not mean the policy was necessarily a legitimate part of the substantive requirements of the Voting Rights Act. Therefore, Georgia's congressional apportionment was unconstitutional.

Texas, too, had acted in part to satisfy a perceived Justice Department minority maximization policy. The legislature had drawn the state's congressional, senate, and House of Representative districts in the urban areas using census blocks, and the districts were bizarre and grotesque in appearance. It was not long before the state was back in federal court defending these plans against the claim that they were unconstitutional racial gerrymanders.

Vera v. Bush was filed by Republicans in January 1994, alleging that the parts of the congressional districts drawn in Dallas and Harris Counties were drawn unconstitutionally on the basis of race and were "racial gerrymanders." A district court consisting of District Judges David Hittner and Melinda Harmon and 5th Circuit Court of Appeals Judge Edith Jones agreed. So did the United States Supreme Court (*Bush v. Vera*).

On remand, the district court implemented an interim plan to remedy the unconstitutional districts in Dallas and Harris Counties. This interim plan necessarily affected thirteen congressional districts. In redrawing the boundary of

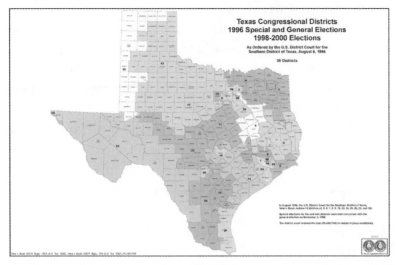

Congressional districts as redrawn by a federal court in 1996. The urban districts were much more regular in appearance than those enacted by the legislature but achieve essentially the same results.

one district to effect a remedy, the boundaries of the contiguous districts are necessarily also changed. Since the 1996 primary elections had used the now unconstitutional districts, the district court voided the results of the primary elections in the thirteen affected districts and ordered a special election in each of these districts on the general election date. Three of these special elections resulted in runoffs, which were conducted on December 10, 1996. These court-drawn congressional districts were used in elections for the remainder of the decade.

Similar federal court challenges were launched against the state legislative apportionment plans in *Thomas v. Bush*. An agreed judgment entered by the court on January 25, 1995, resulted in the redrawing of the offending districts in these state legislative plans. The Texas Legislature quickly enacted the agreed senate plan. A few minor changes were adopted to the agreed court plan for the House of Representatives. The changes were precleared and became legally enforceable for elections during the remainder of the decade.

The resulting districts in all of these court plans (congressional and state legislative districts) were more compact and less unsightly than their predecessors because they were drawn on the basis of election precincts rather than census blocks, but the actual percentages of minority voters in the affected districts changed little. Similarly, the new shapes did little ultimately to change the racial, ethnic, or political nature of the districts.

EFFECTS

The effects of the 1991 congressional plan on minority representation were immediate. An African American was elected to Congress for the first time from Dallas in 1993, raising the number of African Americans in the Texas congressional delegation to two. The number of Hispanic members of Congress from Texas increased from four to five after the 1992 elections and to six by the end of the decade, including one Republican. A congressional district (29) was drawn in Harris County in 1991 with a majority Hispanic population, but its voters elected a non-Hispanic white in 1992 and for the remainder of the decade. A Hispanic Democrat was elected from the district in 2018 after the non-Hispanic white retired.

The 1990s saw substantial growth in Republican strength in all elections. No Democrat won a statewide election after 1994. George W. Bush unseated Ann Richards as governor in that year. In the state legislature and in the state's congressional delegation, the number of Republicans steadily climbed.

One by one, the seats occupied by Democratic incumbents in Texas fell. Sometimes the Democratic incumbent was defeated in election by a Republican. For example, Democrat congressman Bill Sarpalius was defeated by Republican Mac Thornberry in 1994. Just as often, however, the Republicans prevailed in elections to replace retiring Democratic incumbents, including Democratic senators John Montford ('96 special election), Bill Sims ('96 general election), and Jim Turner ('97 special election, when Turner retired to run for Congress). Perhaps reflective of the impact of the *Terrazas* court's redistricting plan for the senate (in contrast to the plan adopted by the legislature), the number of Republican senators increased from eight in 1991 to thirteen after the 1992 election. By 1997, Republicans constituted a majority of the Texas Senate, with sixteen members. Republicans held this majority as the decade ended.

Nevertheless, despite the significant growth in Republican electoral strength statewide, the decade ended with less than a Republican majority in the state House (seventy-eight Democrats to seventy-two Republicans) and in the congressional delegation (seventeen Democrats to thirteen Republicans).

CHAPTER 7

REPUBLICAN

ASCENSION

(2001–2010)

BY 2001, DEMOCRATIC CONTROL OF state government in Texas had ended. No Democrat won a statewide election after 1994. Republicans now held all twenty-nine of the offices elected statewide. The governor of Texas, Rick Perry, was Republican. He had succeeded George W. Bush when Bush was elected president of the United States. Republicans also had a majority of the seats in the Texas Senate. The Democrats, however, still had a majority of the seats in the Texas House of Representatives and of the state's congressional delegation.

This division of power at the state level dictated the strategies and events of 2001. Neither political party expected to be able to pass any apportionment bill that was particularly favorable to their own party's candidates. Not surprisingly, therefore, no apportionment legislation at all won legislative approval.

The state was apportioned two new congressional seats, bringing the total to thirty-two. For Democrats, the failure to pass a congressional redistricting plan was potentially advantageous because the task passed to the courts, and the Democrats could argue that under *Weiser* the courts should defer to the state policy embodied in the existing congressional district plan and largely maintain the status quo. Such an outcome could be expected to leave the Democrats with an ability to retain a majority of the Texas congressional delegation.

This legislative inaction, however, proved disastrous for the Democrats in the House and senate because responsibility for redistricting the state legislative seats passed to the LRB. For Republicans, this predictable outcome was advantageous for state legislative districts because four of the five members of the board were Republican. Some feel that this legislative inaction was not a result of any legislative gridlock but was from the beginning part of a Republican plan to seize control of the Texas House in 2002 in gerrymandered districts drawn by the LRB in 2001 and to use the Republican majority in both the House and senate to redraw congressional districts in 2003.

STATE LEGISLATIVE DISTRICTS

In hindsight, there is good reason to believe that no opportunity for legislative compromise existed in 2001 because the Republican leaders wanted the issue to go to the LRB.

The Democrats had a plan for dealing with the Republican-controlled LRB. The strategy was not totally unreasonable. The lone Democrat on the LRB, Speaker of the Texas House of Representatives James E. "Pete" Laney, fought to maintain or enhance Democratic strength. His plan proposed to reduce the percentage of minority voters in the safe minority districts and redistribute these voters among other competitive districts to enhance the chances of Democratic candidates in those districts.

As a consultant to the LRB, I thought that the safe minority (especially African American) districts could be reduced in minority percentage without endangering the minority incumbents, but I thought it would require the DOJ to accept a new legal theory, would encounter the opposition of some minorities, and was an unwise action for the LRB. The lieutenant governor, Bill Ratliff, who had been elected as a senator and succeeded Rick Perry as lieutenant governor when Perry became governor, was Republican but favored apportionment plans, especially for the senate, that avoided major partisan changes that could endanger incumbents and disrupt the legislature. This gave Democrats potentially two of the five votes on the LRB. They only needed one more.

The additional vote was never forthcoming. A majority of three members of the LRB wanted a reapportionment favoring Republican candidates. Attorney General John Cornyn served as chairman of the commission and led the battle for apportionment plans, especially in the House of Representatives, which were legal but likely to defeat Democratic incumbents and give Republicans full control of the Texas Legislature.

I understood my duty to be to advise each member of the board on a plan's legality, not on its partisan implications. Several of Cornyn's plans were ones that I considered likely to receive a DOJ objection; I advised the LRB accordingly. Cornyn withdrew the plans and reworked his House and senate plans to address the problems I had identified. Eventually, he proposed plans that I thought would gain preclearance. Cornyn was always professional with me and respectful of my legal opinions, but this was not true of some of his assistants who seemed much more interested in furthering the political future of Cornyn than in meeting legal requirements. I resigned when the LRB adjourned, and in my letter of resignation to Cornyn I called these assistants "twerps."

Many alternative plans were considered for both chambers of the legislature, including one that targeted Speaker Pete Laney for defeat. The final LRB apportionment plans were adopted by a 3–2 vote, with Speaker Laney and Lieutenant Governor Bill Ratliff dissenting. Although Ratliff dissented, his alternative plans for the senate had significantly affected the shape of the final plan for that chamber. By contrast, Speaker Laney's House plan had little or no effect on the LRB's House plan.

The LRB plans were submitted for preclearance to a DOJ that was now within a Republican (George W. Bush) administration. The senate plan won approval. The plan for the House of Representatives did not. The DOJ found that the House plan caused a retrogression of Hispanic voting strength in two predominantly Hispanic districts. A last-minute amendment at the LRB explained as an effort to prevent Laney's reelection caused a redrawing of other West Texas districts and resulted in the Hispanic percentage dropping in District 74 along the Mexican border. I had missed this potential retrogression. The state quickly agreed to modify these districts to meet the DOJ objections and an agreed judgment was entered in federal court redrawing these Hispanic districts and maintaining the remainder of the LRB plan. These state senate and House of Representatives district plans remained in effect for the remainder of the decade.

CONGRESSIONAL DISTRICTS: STATE COURT

The partisan fight over congressional districts in Texas started early and lasted until 2006. It attracted worldwide attention.

Democratic strategy in 2001 was dictated largely by attorneys because favorable legislative action appeared highly unlikely. Even if a favorable apportionment plan could be passed through the divided legislature, such a plan could not avoid a gubernatorial veto. At the same time, it was clear that the existing congressional districts, which had been drawn in the previous decade on the basis of the 1990 census, were invalid because unequal in population. Further, there were two new districts that needed to be added, necessitating an entirely new map. Therefore, the Democrats began jockeying early for a favorable judicial forum to adopt a new plan. The first federal lawsuit from the Democrats was filed on December 28, 2000, even before the legislature convened. A sister state lawsuit had been filed a day earlier in district court in Travis County.

Not to be outdone, the Republicans soon filed their own federal and state lawsuits in a search for a favorable forum. The Mexican American Legal Defense and Educational Fund also initiated federal court litigation. Altogether there were five federal and five state cases filed. Despite the presence of this litigation and the obvious difficulty inherent in the legislature passing a congressional redistricting, some in the legislature tried. Lieutenant Governor Ratliff appointed Republican senator Jeff Wentworth to chair the senate redistricting committee. Wentworth obtained some bipartisan support for a compromise plan that probably increased the number of Republican seats but generally preserved all congressional incumbents. Wentworth's efforts to implement a compromise congressional plan failed.

The state filed motions to dismiss the early lawsuits as premature. Three of the federal lawsuits were dismissed. It soon became apparent, however, that the legislature was not going to act. Governor Perry said he would call a special session on congressional redistricting but only if "acceptable plans" existed. No special session occurred. As a result, the battle over congressional districts actively shifted to the courts.

The Democrats wanted a state district court in Travis County, where all the district judges were Democrats, to decide congressional redistricting. The Republicans wanted the decisions made by a state district court in Harris County, where all the district judges were Republican. For months during the summer of 2001, the lawyers journeyed back and forth between these courts and the appellate courts, wrangling over which state district court had jurisdiction.

Ultimately, the Texas Supreme Court resolved the jurisdictional dispute. When both district courts tried to proceed simultaneously, the Texas Supreme Court on September 7 stayed both hearings. The court then stepped in to settle the jurisdictional dispute (*Perry v. DelRio*). The court found that the adjournment of the regular legislative session provided a "bright line" for determining the ripeness of lawsuits challenging congressional redistricting. It found that jurisdiction is not bestowed by a lawsuit filed before this date but could be created by an amendment to such a suit after the legislature adjourned. After reviewing the history of the pending state cases, the court held that the first case filed after the legislative session was in Travis County. Therefore, the Travis County district court had jurisdiction over congressional redistricting.

Trial commenced immediately (September 17) in the Travis County district court. All the many interests were represented. Alternative redistricting plans were abundant. The court appointed the Texas Legislative Council as its expert to assist in coming up with a satisfactory plan. On October 3, 2001, the state court issued its order adopting a congressional redistricting plan.

House Speaker Pete Laney, however, petitioned the court for some substantive changes to the plan. The court agreed to Laney's changes, which essentially resulted in the adoption of a new plan. The Republicans were outraged at this last bit of maneuvering. The state, represented by Texas Attorney General John Cornyn, was also upset. Both appealed, along with Congressman Tom DeLay and others, to the Texas Supreme Court.

The Texas Supreme Court rejected the attorney general's argument that he was the "state" for purposes of submitting a redistricting plan and that the district court was required to accept the state's plan. The court found, however, that the AG has the authority to propose and suggest redistricting plans when appropriate to a court but does not have the authority on his own to redistrict the state. Nevertheless, the court found that the Travis County district court had erred by failing to provide a meaningful hearing on the plan submitted by Speaker Laney. Therefore, the state court's apportionment plan was a nullity (that is, legally void). Time had run out for Democrats in the state courts again.

CONGRESSIONAL DISTRICTS: FEDERAL COURT

The federal lawsuits challenging the state's lack of a new congressional redistricting plan had been consolidated before a three-judge court (*Balderas v. Texas*). The court consisted of District Judges John Hannah and John Ward and 5th Circuit Judge Patrick Higginbotham. As dictated by *Growe v. Emison*, the federal court stayed its hand to give state institutions, including the state courts, an opportunity to enact a lawful districting plan. The federal court waited as the proceedings played out in state court. After the Texas Supreme Court's determination that the Travis County district court's plan was a nullity, however, the federal court began its own hearing.

The federal court felt bound by precedent (*Weiser*) to start with the existing congressional districts and to make only those changes necessary to bring that plan into compliance with the applicable law. This legal requirement benefited the Democrats in this instance, but in other instances it has benefited Republicans. For example, the Supreme Court's reversal in January 2012 of the district court's interim plan in *Perez v. Perry* was based on this same principle. So was the decision of the Supreme Court in 1981 in *Upham v. Seamon*.

The court adopted a redistricting plan that incorporated the two new congressional seats into the areas of greatest population growth: one was located in the Dallas–Fort Worth metroplex and the other linked Austin to western Harris County. Both new districts eventually elected Republicans. The plan then equalized population among all the districts and essentially maintained as much as possible the existing "member-constituent relations."

The state, represented by Attorney General John Cornyn, was accepting of the court's approach. Some Republicans always looked at the court-drawn plan as an interim plan that would be replaced by a more Republican one drawn by the 2003 legislature. I do not know Cornyn's personal view. The state had presented Rice University professor John Alford as an expert witness and designer of the plan. An analysis of the voting patterns in the districts showed that most of the districts with non-Hispanic white Democratic incumbent congressmen would vote Republican. Even Congressman Tom DeLay hailed the result. Democratic lawyers were pleased, however, because they felt that the combination of Democratic incumbency and the lack of strong Republican candidates in the district races would allow the Democratic incumbents to survive.

The 2002 elections were conducted using the court's plan. Incumbency proved to be a big factor in victories. As Democratic lawyers had predicted, the Democratic incumbents in these districts all won reelection in 2002. This outcome was a surprise and angered some Republicans, especially those in Washington who had counted on the votes of these Republicans to aid in Congress. Different theories about the situation exist. One is that Republican officials never expected Republicans to prevail over incumbent Democrats in 2002 under the court plan and were planning all along to change these congressional districts in 2003 once they had a House majority. Another theory is that the court was pro-Democrat and intentionally imposed a plan that favored Democratic incumbents. Republicans utilized this latter theory as one of the reasons for "payback" in 2003.

STATE LEGISLATIVE AND CONGRESSIONAL ELECTIONS IN 2002

In state legislative elections in 2002, the story was very different. Several organizations, including Tom DeLay's political action committee Texans for a Republican Majority (TRMPAC), raised and spent money to help the Republicans gain a majority of the Texas House of Representatives. This effort proved successful and, taking advantage of the opportunity presented by the LRB's partisan drawing of House districts, Republicans gained a majority of seats (88) in the 150-member Texas House of Representatives for the first time in 130 years.

In its development effort to support Republican candidates in 2002, however, TRMPAC aggressively solicited money from the treasuries of corporations. The Texas Election Code prohibited the use of such funds on behalf of candidates for office except "to finance the establishment or administration" of a political action committee (PAC). Whether TRMPAC's aggressive solicitation and use of corporate funds was illegal under Texas law eventually became less relevant after the United States Supreme Court in *Citizens United v. FEC* (2010) found that corporations have a constitutional right to make independent expenditures to expressly support or oppose candidates.

DeLay and TRMPAC were not immediately off the hook, though. Even *Citizens United* apparently allows governments, including that of the State of Texas, to continue to prohibit corporations from contributing to candidates. One TRMPAC action seemed to be a violation of this prohibition. TRMPAC had been cautious not to contribute corporate funds directly to any candidate. Anxious to see a Republican victory in 2002, however, TRMPAC, in September of that year, agreed to give

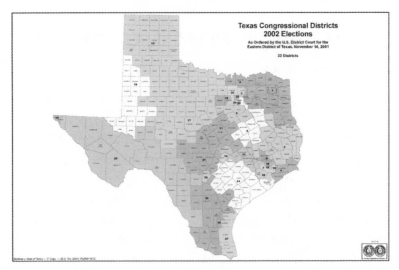

Congressional districts for the 2002 elections, as ordered by federal district court when the Texas Legislature failed to enact any congressional plan.

$190,000 of its corporate ("soft") money to the Republican National Committee (RNC) in return for the RNC contributing the same amount in "hard" money directly to specific Republican candidates that TRMPAC wanted to win in the Texas House of Representatives.

Democrats felt that TRMPAC's agreement with the RNC was an obvious attempt to avoid the Texas Election Code prohibition. Once this trade of monies became known to the district attorney of Travis County, felony indictments were returned against two of DeLay's associates, Jim Ellis and John Colyandro, after the election and, in 2005, against DeLay himself. This indictment forced DeLay out of his position of majority leader in the United States House of Representatives. In 2006, DeLay resigned from Congress. After many years of legal jockeying, a jury in 2010 convicted former congressman DeLay of felony money laundering and conspiracy, but this conviction was overturned on appeal.

After the 2002 elections, Democrats lost their majority in the Texas House but still held a 17 to 15 edge in the state's congressional delegation. With their new majority in the House of Representatives, however, the Republicans were positioned for the first time to change this ratio in the state's congressional delegation. Republican Tom Craddick's election as Speaker of the Texas House of Representatives seemed to ensure Republican success.

THE 2003 CONGRESSIONAL REDISTRICTING

There was no legal necessity for changing the congressional plan that had been used in the 2002 election. In the past, the legislature had let court-ordered plans become permanent or adopted the court's plan as its own in legislation.

Pressure for a change in congressional district boundaries in 2003 came from Washington, DC. Some still feel that redistricting in 2003 to defeat Democratic incumbents was always part of the Republican master plan and not a result of any immediate pressure from Washington Republicans who held only a slim majority in the United States House of Representatives. As a result, several of President George W. Bush's major programs, such as tax cuts, the estate tax repeal, etc., narrowly survived procedural votes. More Republicans were needed in Congress. Several opportunities were identified for possibly redrawing congressional district boundaries to elect more Republicans. Texas was the gold mine, with a potential addition of an estimated four to eight seats for Republicans. Congressman Tom DeLay took the lead on behalf of the Republican members of the Texas congressional delegation and the White House to gain these seats.

Republican officials in Texas agreed in 2003 to redraw the state's congressional districts. Some state Republicans at first resisted the change, but this dynamic changed when then newly elected Attorney General Gregory Abbott issued an official opinion that, since the congressional plan used for elections in 2002 had been court-ordered, the Texas Legislature had a duty to adopt legislation that redrew the district boundaries and had the legislature's imprimatur. This opinion was crucial because it changed the dynamic among Republican legislators. Until that point, many legislators had a "you gotta be kidding me" reaction when the unpopular subject of redistricting was broached. Afterward, congressional redistricting became a litmus test of Republican and Democratic loyalty and "duty." Democrats in the Texas House of Representatives and Senate fought to prevent any change.

Democratic efforts in the regular legislative session to stop or seriously amend the Republican congressional redistricting plan were unsuccessful. As the session drew to a close, it was clear that the Republican majority was poised to enact the highly partisan redistricting legislation that would elect at least five new Republicans to Congress. This situation led to the events described in the introduction of this book.

The idea of staging a walkout of Democrats to break the House quorum was first raised in the House Democratic Caucus on May 5, 2003, by Democratic Representative Richard Raymond. (As with most legislative bodies, there must be a quorum present for the body to enact legislation. The Texas Constitution sets the quorum for the Texas House of Representatives at two-thirds of its members.) There was no consensus at the meeting that it would work. After the meeting, Caucus Chairman Jim Dunnam pondered the options. There were no good choices, but a walkout that lasted past adjournment on May 15 would, under House rules, prevent the redistricting bill (a House bill) from being considered. The rule prevents consideration of a House bill after the 123rd day of a session. The rule can be suspended, but only by the vote of two-thirds of the members present. Dunnam was confident that he could muster the votes needed to prevent the rule from being suspended.

In a masterpiece of skullduggery, the organization of fifty-one or more Democrats to leave Texas occurred in secret. Democratic Representative Ron Wilson was not asked to participate in the walkout because he favored the Republican legislation. He insists that he and the Republicans knew about the walkout beforehand, but this claim is contradicted by Craddick's reaction when he discovered that the Democrats had left. Of course, there is the possibility that Republicans had heard a rumor about the walkout but doubted the Democrats could actually make it happen.

The caper could be costly for each participant because they could possibly be forfeiting the opportunity to pass their own legislation at the end of the session, and each participant could expect to feel the future retribution of Speaker Craddick. Eventually, though, Dunnam had enough members to commit for his walkout to work. On Sunday, May 11, Dunnam and forty-six other Democrats rode buses to Ardmore, Oklahoma, out of reach of any Texas state troopers sent to fetch them. They arrived at about 1:30 a.m. Another six Democrats used other transportation to leave the state. Some traveled to Oklahoma. Former House Speaker Pete Laney flew his own plane to Ardmore.

Eventually, Dunnam had fifty-two Democrats, counting himself, housed two to a room at a Holiday Inn in Ardmore. The accommodations were cramped but adequate. The Democrats had pulled off the walkout. A fiasco for the Party had been averted and the House was now without a quorum.

The first official evidence of the Democrats' departure came on Monday morning when the House was convened. It was filled with Republicans and a few Democrats but, lacking a quorum, could not enact legislation. The initial Republican reaction was one of disbelief combined with frantic activity. According to Governor Perry's chief of staff, Mike Toomey, "everyone" was involved in trying to find the missing Democrats. Speaker Craddick "locked down" the

House to keep anyone else from leaving. A "call" on the House ostensibly required every member to immediately come to the House chamber.

Warrants were issued for the arrest of each missing Democrat; these warrants were addressed to "all Peace Officers" in the state. Attorney General Abbott assured the Department of Public Safety that its officers could make the arrests. These warrants resulted in surveillance of some of the Democrats' homes but no arrests. Governor Perry's office contacted the Republican governor of New Mexico to see if arrests could be made in that state in the event the Democrats were there.

Of particular note was the Republican effort to enlist federal assistance. Attorney General Abbott, through his first assistant Barry McBee, called the Department of Justice and asked if the FBI could track down the missing Democrats. Congressman DeLay asked for help from the DOJ and the Federal Aviation Agency (FAA). This latter agency was asked to locate and track former Speaker Laney's private plane. The basic response from the federal agencies to these Republican entreaties was cordial but unenthusiastic. They maintained that the walkout was basically an internal political matter beyond any federal agency's jurisdiction.

Eventually, the missing Democrats in Ardmore were located by the Republicans, but there was no official way to get them back to Austin. Some effort was made by cell phone to persuade individual Democrats in Ardmore to return to Austin, but none did so. After several days of partisan stand-off, the two sides agreed to a truce. The Democrats would return, the House would continue with its normal business until the regular session ended on June 1, and the Republicans would not try to enact the redistricting legislation. On May 16, the missing Democrats rejoined their Republican colleagues. The regular session ended on June 1, 2003, without redrawing the state's congressional districts. The walkout had been a success for the Democrats.

This Democratic victory was short-lived. The Republicans had been embarrassed but not defeated. On June 16, a crucial strategy meeting was held at the Governor's Mansion with Governor Perry, Lieutenant Governor David Dewhurst, Speaker Craddick, and Congressman DeLay in attendance. Their decision was to try again to pass a new congressional redistricting plan. Shortly thereafter, Governor Perry called a special session of the legislature to begin on June 30, 2003, with the primary subject being congressional redistricting.

Once the special session began, it became clear that the Democrats in the House were not likely to repeat their walkout. The members were concerned about a public backlash if they walked out again and realized that the Republicans now had the upper hand. If anything could be done to stop the Republican juggernaut, it would have to be done by the Democrats in the senate.

The circumstances in the senate appeared more favorable for Democrats than they had been in the House. The Republican presiding officer, newly elected Lieutenant Governor Dewhurst, was generally liked by most Democratic senators and was seen as less partisan than Speaker Craddick. He would prove, however, to be more calculating and intractable than the Democrats' adversary in the House.

The Democrats wanted Dewhurst to apply the so-called two-thirds rule[3] to prevent any redistricting legislation being reached on the senate calendar without a two-thirds vote. Application of this requirement would effectively mean that no legislation could pass without some Democratic support. Dewhurst agreed to apply the two-thirds vote requirement because he expected to win one or more Democratic votes.

---

3. This is a misnomer, as there was never any actual "two-thirds rule." For years, the senate had required a suspension of the rules (i.e., an affirmative vote of two-thirds of the members present) to take up legislation that was not at the top of the senate calendar. Usually in a special session, a suspension of the rules is not required to reach legislation because there are few bills on the calendar. The senate rules were changed in 2015 to replace "two-thirds" with "three-fifths."

Instead, several Republican senators balked at supporting redistricting legislation they considered "distasteful." The leader of the senate Democrats, John Whitmire, could muster only ten votes to block consideration of the redistricting legislation. Republican Bill Ratliff gave him the needed eleventh vote. It became clear that the special session, which is limited by the constitution to thirty days, would end without redistricting legislation. Dewhurst, however, indicated that he would not enforce a two-thirds vote requirement in any future special session.

Republicans hoped to prevent senate Democrats from a walkout like that of their House counterparts. Their strategy was to end the first thirty-day special session a day early, to immediately call a second special session, to close the senate chamber doors to keep anyone from leaving, and to trap the Democratic senators in the senate chamber to guarantee a quorum for a second special session. Governor Perry announced a second session, but it was too late. The senate Democrats had gotten wind of the Republican plan of entrapment and had boarded a private plane for Albuquerque, New Mexico. One Democrat, Senator Ken Armbrister, stayed behind. With the departure of eleven Democrats, however, the senate lacked a quorum for the newly called second special session.

In some ways, the senators had it easier in Albuquerque than the House Democrats had in Ardmore: the accommodations were better, the city was larger and offered more attractions, the senators could travel around New Mexico without fear of arrest, many staff members were present, and some senators had visits from their families. Unlike with the House walkout, however, there was no clear end game.

The standoff continued for weeks. Dewhurst had tried to convince the Democrats not to leave. Now, he resisted pressure from Republicans to denigrate the Democrats and tried in person or through trusted emissaries to convince the

Democrats to return. He would not, however, agree to reinstate a two-thirds vote requirement for consideration of the redistricting legislation. The second special session ended with the Democrats still in Albuquerque, but Governor Perry indicated that he would call as many special sessions as "necessary" to pass the redistricting legislation.

All summer, the Democrats had been told by their attorneys that rescinding the two-thirds vote requirement without federal preclearance was a violation of Section 5 of the Voting Rights Act. With negotiations with Dewhurst showing no progress, the Democrats filed a lawsuit on August 11 based on this theory and asked a federal district court in Laredo to enjoin the state. Even though probably a Democrat, the judge was skeptical. No temporary restraining order was forthcoming. The DOJ by letter asserted that rescission of the two-thirds vote requirement was not a violation of the Voting Rights Act. A three-judge court was convened. One day after hearing argument, the court on September 18, 2003, unanimously rejected the Democrats' claim (*Barrientos v. State*).

All it would take to establish a quorum in the senate for a third special session was the return to Texas of a single Democratic senator. Initially, the Democrats were united and even went through the process of meeting each day on legislative issues, but by the end of thirty days many of the Democrats were tired and ready to go home. The discouraging progress of the *Barrientos* litigation brought an atmosphere of gloom. The first Democratic senator known to return to Texas was John Whitmire. By September 3, he was home to stay in Houston. The walkout was effectively over. Other senate Democrats criticized Whitmire, but most soon followed him to Texas.

A third special session began on September 15. Under the leadership of Congressman Tom DeLay, the Republicans were able to craft a highly partisan plan that was intended to defeat all ten of the non-Hispanic white Democratic incumbents in Congress from Texas. One effect of the drawn-out partisan battle was that the Republican goal of adding four to six Republicans to Congress had evolved to defeating all ten of the non-Hispanic Democratic incumbents and adding white Republican voters to District 23 to help the Republican incumbent prevail in a majority Hispanic district.

The carefully constructed gerrymanders were designed to personally defeat each of these congressmen. DeLay acknowledged that his plan targeted only the Anglo (i.e., non-Hispanic white) Democratic incumbents so that it could avoid the possibility of a DOJ objection under Section 5 of the Voting Rights Act. If a district had a majority, or near majority, of African American or Hispanic voters but elected an Anglo or a Republican, DeLay considered it to be "nonperforming" and susceptible to change. The only districts that met this definition were Districts 23, 24, and 29. With regard to District 29 in Harris County, the configuration of the district remained essentially unchanged but with the residence of the Anglo incumbent left outside the redrawn district.

In regard to Dallas County's District 24, which was over 50 percent minority but not a majority of either African American or Hispanic voters, the urge to defeat Democratic incumbent Martin Frost led DeLay to convince the legislature to break up the existing district and to make the new district Republican. District 23 was majority Hispanic. It ran along the Mexico border in West Texas, but a Republican had won it in a tight race. The ultimate plan in 2003 changed the configuration of District 23 by adding non-Hispanic white voters northwest of Bexar County to help the Republican incumbent win reelection. The changes to Districts 23 and 24 were challenged in court. The US Supreme Court struck down the changes to District 23 as violating Section 2 of the Voting Rights Act.

Eventually, eight of the ten non-Hispanic white Democratic incumbents were not returned to Congress as Democrats. It played out like so:

Democrat Max Sandlin won election in 2002 in District 1 with 56 percent of the vote. The district was redrawn in 2003 and he lost his bid for reelection in 2004.

Democrat Jim Turner won reelection in 2002 in District 2 with 61 percent of the vote. The district was redrawn in 2003 by: (1) moving Turner's residence and home county (Houston County) out of the district; (2) scattering the remainder of the old District 2 among multiple districts; (3) putting Turner's residence and rural county in a district that ran 200 miles to the north to a heavily populated suburban area with a Republican incumbent (Pete Sessions); and (4) renumbering the district as District 6. Turner did not seek reelection. As a result, the Republican incumbent moved over to challenge Frost. The new District 2 was in the southeast corner of the state.

Democrat Ralph Hall in District 4 switched parties and won reelection as a Republican in 2004.

Democrat Nick Lampson won reelection in 2002 in District 9 with 59 percent of the vote. The district was renumbered as District 2 and redrawn to extend into heavily Republican areas near Houston. Lampson lost his reelection bid in 2004.

Democrat Chet Edwards won reelection in 2002 in District 11 with 52 percent of the vote. The district was renumbered District 17 and stretched to include suburban areas near Tarrant and Dallas Counties on the north and areas near Harris County on the south. Nevertheless, Edwards won reelection in 2004 over a Texas House Republican for whom the district was designed and again in 2006 and 2008. He finally lost in 2010.

Democrat Charles Stenholm won reelection in 2002 in West Texas District 17 with 52 percent of the vote when Democratic statewide candidates were losing with only 28 percent of the vote in the district. District 17 was renumbered as District 19 and was carefully reconfigured to exclude areas that had voted for Stenholm in the past and to include the City of Lubbock and a Republican incumbent (Randy Neugebauer) on the west end. Stenholm ran for reelection in 2004 but lost.

Democrat Lloyd Doggett was first elected to Congress in 1994. He was the incumbent in District 10. The district was primarily in Travis County (Austin) and strongly Democratic. The 2003 redistricting split Travis County. The county ended up being a small part of five districts. Doggett's old District 10 was made Republican by stretching it 200 miles to include some Houston suburbs. A new District 25 was: (1) drawn to exclude Doggett's residence; (2) configured to include only a sliver, primarily Hispanic, of Travis County; and (3) stretched 300 miles to the Rio Grande. However, it was likely to elect a Democrat. The elongated district was nicknamed the "walking stick district" by justices on the US Supreme Court. Republicans thought it likely that Doggett would not run for reelection, would be defeated by a Republican in redrawn District 10, or would be defeated in the Democratic primary in District 25 by a Hispanic where the population of the district was 78.3 percent Hispanic. Doggett ran for election in the new District 25. He won in 2004 and continued to serve into 2019.

Democrat Martin Frost was the incumbent in congressional District 24. He had served in Congress for twenty-three years and was the leader of the Texas Democratic congressional delegation. In Congressman DeLay's view, Frost had to go. Initially, the Republican leaders endorsed the idea of making District 24 into a majority Hispanic district, with the hope that Frost would lose in the Democratic primary. DeLay soon realized, however, that Frost would probably win such a district. He urged a plan to pack Hispanics into the neighboring heavily African American District 30. This made it 76.1 percent minority and divided the other African American and Hispanic communities among five other now heavily Republican districts. The Democratic incumbent in District 30 was African American Congresswoman Eddie Bernice Johnson. District 24 was reconfigured without most of its previous minority population. Frost ran for reelection in 2004 in a new District 32 but lost to Republican Pete Sessions. Sessions had been an incumbent in District 5, which had been joined with District 6, but once it became clear that the Democratic incumbent (Jim Turner) would not seek reelection, Sessions decided to oppose Frost in the new District 32.

Democrat Chris Bell was elected overwhelmingly in 2002 in District 25. The district was reconfigured to draw African Americans from nearby districts and renumbered as District 9. Bell lost in the Democratic primary in 2004 to African American Al Green.

Democrat Gene Green was the incumbent in District 29. The district was majority Hispanic, but Green had represented the district since 1992. The 2003 redistricting plan removed Green's residence from the district. However, a member of Congress is not required to live in his or her district and Green ran successfully for reelection in District 29 in 2004. He continued to serve as congressman until his retirement in 2018.

The new congressional redistricting plan won DOJ pre-clearance (a memo was later discovered that showed that the DOJ staff had recommended that the DOJ interpose a Section 5 objection to the plan but that political appointees of the Bush administration had overruled the staff) but was challenged in federal court. A new three-judge court, with two members remaining from the *Balderas* court, heard these challenges. The federal district court rejected all claims and the 2004 congressional elections were held using the districts in the legislation. The United States Supreme Court later remanded the case for further hearings after its ruling in *Vieth v. Jubelirer* on partisan gerrymandering.

The district court again upheld the 2003 redistricting plan. This time on appeal, the US Supreme Court agreed with the lower court's rejection of the partisan gerrymandering allegations but found that the legislature had violated Section 2 of the Voting Rights Act in its redrawing of District 23 by splitting the heavily Hispanic Laredo, reducing the Hispanic percentage in the district, and adding the staunchly Republican "hill country" to the district (*League of United Latin American Citizens v. Perry*). Justice Kennedy called the state's map "an affront and an insult" to Texas's minority voters. On behalf of the Supreme Court, he held that "the State took away the Latinos' opportunity because Latinos were about to exercise it. This bears the mark of intentional discrimination that could give rise to an equal protection violation." On remand, the federal district court redrew the boundaries of District 23, and those of five other districts, to remedy the violation.

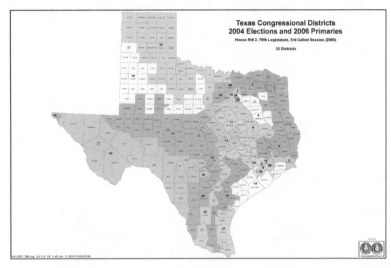

Congressional districts following the 2003 re-redistricting and used for the 2004 elections and 2006 primaries until invalidated by *League of Latin American Citizens v. Perry*.

Several of the districts in this configuration were subsequently redrawn by the district court for the 2006 election because District 23 (running along the Mexico border in West Texas) was found by the US Supreme Court to violate the Voting Rights Act by being redrawn in 2003 to include Anglo areas on its east for the ostensible purpose of protecting a Republican incumbent, Henry Bonilla. The court's remedial redrawing of District 23 caused the reconfiguration of several nearby districts, including District 25 (represented by Lloyd Doggett) for the 2006 elections.

The 2003 congressional redistricting plan was, as I testified in DeLay's criminal trial, a "masterful gerrymander." Each district in the plan was carefully designed to defeat one of the ten incumbent non-Hispanic white Democratic congressmen or to reelect a Republican congressman. By the end of the decade, only two of the ten non-Hispanic white Democrats targeted in the 2003 redistricting survived. Republicans outnumbered Democrats in the congressional delegation 23–9.

DeLay also had a longer-term objective. He wanted non-Hispanic white voters and potential candidates to see the Democratic Party as made up primarily of minority voters and officials and unwelcoming to others. The defeat of all the non-Hispanic white officeholders would advance that objective by making all Democratic congressmen from Texas either African American or Hispanic.[4]

EFFECTS

The decade of the 2000s was the culmination of a sea change in Texas politics. In 2001, the Democrats, faced with a diminished electoral base, had miscalculated in regard to the LRB, the state court system, the DOJ (under George W. Bush), and the federal courts. They no longer had majorities in the House or the senate. The Democratic majority in the congressional seats survived only until the 2004 elections.

By the middle of the decade, Republicans controlled most of the institutions of state government. All the statewide offices, including governor, lieutenant governor, and attorney general, were held by Republicans. The Republicans had gained a majority of the members of the House of Representatives to add to their majority in the senate.

The congressional redistricting in 2003 resulted in the defeat, resignation, or party change of eight Democratic incumbents. One of the three survivors lost in 2010. One of these incumbents was replaced by another Democrat. One of these deposed Democrats (Nick Lampson) temporarily won the seat vacated by Tom DeLay in 2006 but then lost it again in 2008. On the other hand, the Democrats won congressional District 23 from Republican Henry Bonilla in 2006 after

---

4. If the reader wishes to learn more about these events, please read my book, *Lines in the Sand: Congressional Redistricting in Texas and the Downfall of Tom DeLay* (University of Texas Press, 2007).

the three-judge federal court redrew the district, only to lose it again in 2010.

The last election of the decade in 2010 brought a Republican tsunami in the House elections. Democrats over the decade had gradually regained some of the Texas House of Representatives seats lost in 2002 and, although still a minority in the House, numbered seventy-four representatives. Republicans knocked off twenty-three of these in the 2010 election. After two representatives just reelected as Democrats changed political parties, the Democrats found themselves with only forty-nine seats out of 150 (Republicans with 101) going into the 2011 legislative session. The 2010 election brought no changes in the makeup of the Texas Senate, but left Republicans with a majority (19–12).

Republicans unseated three Democratic incumbent congressmen (Chet Edwards, Solomon Ortiz, and Ciro Rodriguez) in 2010. Two of these were in districts with Hispanic majorities. As of 2011, Republicans held twenty-three of the existing thirty-two congressional seats. The cumulative effect of these Republican victories set the stage for complete domination by Republicans of redistricting by the legislature in 2011.

CHAPTER 8

REPUBLICAN DOMINANCE (2011–2019)

AN UNCERTAIN LEGAL ENVIRONMENT CASTS a shadow over the period discussed in this chapter. Three US Supreme Court decisions during the decade significantly changed the rules for redistricting, and the litigation challenging the Texas Legislature's enactments continued for the entire decade.

The effects of one of these decisions (*Shelby County v. Holder*) were felt in Texas immediately. The potential effects of the second case (*Evenwel v. Abbott*) may prove significant for the future. The third case (*Rucho v. Common Cause*) is a landmark decision but likely will have little practical impact on the outcome of Texas cases.

The litigation challenging the legislative enactments (*Perez v. Perry*) began in 2011, was active throughout the decade, and finally ended after eight years, in 2019, when the district court denied the plaintiffs' request to subject the state to a continuing preclearance requirement.

SHELBY COUNTY V. HOLDER: NO MORE DOJ PRECLEARANCE REVIEW UNDER THE VOTING RIGHTS ACT

Texas had chafed under Section 5 of the Voting Rights Act since it first became subject to the section's preclearance requirements in 1975. On at least two occasions, the state had responded to pending lawsuits by filing answers that included claims that the section was unconstitutional, but the state had resolved the lawsuits without following through on these claims. Republicans in Texas generally pushed for holding the preclearance requirement unconstitutional. Democrats generally opposed such a finding.

In 2011, Shelby County, Alabama, sued the US attorney general in the US District Court in Washington, DC, seeking a declaratory judgment that Sections 4(b) and 5 of the Voting Rights Act were facially unconstitutional and requesting a permanent injunction against their enforcement. The district court upheld the provisions. On June 25, 2013, the US Supreme Court ruled in the case by a 5–4 vote that Section 4(b) was unconstitutional because the coverage formula in the section was based on data over forty years old, making it no longer responsive to current needs and therefore an impermissible burden on the constitutional principles of federalism and equal sovereignty of the states. The court did not strike down Section 5, but without Section 4(b), there was no mechanism or formula for making any jurisdiction subject to Section 5 preclearance.

Whether the finding in *Shelby County* will be ultimately beneficial to the Republican Party in Texas remains to be determined. Many national leaders of the Party, such as Bob Dole, had taken a major role in previously retaining and strengthening the Voting Rights Act. Also, some observers felt that Republicans benefited from the act because the creation of majority-minority districts by packing Democratic voters into a few districts increased Republican strength in the remaining districts. Finally, some Republicans felt that the Party's association with a challenge to Section 5 would make it more difficult in the future to secure the support of Hispanic and African American voters for Republican candidates.

Still, many think the Voting Rights Act outlived its usefulness and that Section 5 of the act was an unacceptable federal intrusion that unfairly burdened Texas and the local governments in this state. The redistricting process in 2021–2022 will largely determine whether the *Shelby* decision benefits the Republican Party in Texas as expected.

EVENWEL V. ABBOTT: POPULATION OR ELIGIBLE VOTERS

In 2016, the United States Supreme Court in *Evenwel v. Abbott*, 578 U.S. (April 4, 2016) upheld the right of Texas to draw its state senate districts using total population numbers from the census. This decision upholding the use of population was no surprise, but the opinion did not foreclose the use of "eligible voters" (i.e., citizen voting age population) in the future.

Two justices (Samuel Alito and Clarence Thomas) concurred in an opinion that jurisdictions could use total population for redistricting but also expressly indicated that it was permissible to use eligible voters. The court as a whole left this issue unresolved in an apparent effort to reach a unanimous decision on a short-handed court. The combined effect of *Evenwel* and *Shelby County* sets the stage for the possibility of a major change in the redistricting process. It is clear that redistricting on the basis of eligible voters instead of population would have been "retrogressive" and objectionable under Section 5 of the Voting Rights Act. Whether such a change also would violate Section 2 of the act remains to be determined now that Section 5 is no longer useable.

RUCHO V. COMMON CAUSE: PARTISAN GERRYMANDERING

In 1986, a majority of the US Supreme Court (*Davis v. Bandemer*) agreed that partisan gerrymandering could violate the US Constitution, but the justices could not agree on a standard to apply to determine "when political gerrymandering has gone too far." During the intervening thirty-three years, not a single federal case had ultimately held a redistricting plan invalid because it was a partisan gerrymander. The issue had been raised in litigation in Texas during every decade from the 1960s, but it was never successful.

The pendency of cases before the Supreme Court in 2018–2019 raised the potential of a possible ruling reaffirming that partisan gerrymandering was justiciable and establishing a standard to use in future litigation. On June 27, 2019, the US Supreme Court by a 5–4 vote held that partisan gerrymandering was a "political question" that was not justiciable in federal court—thus bringing an end to this elusive right. In an opinion written by Chief Justice John Roberts, the court explained, "The practice was known in the Colonies prior to Independence, and the Framers were familiar with it at the time of the drafting and ratification of the Constitution," further noting that election matters had been assigned by the Constitution to the states.

Chief Justice Roberts maintained, "Partisan gerrymandering claims invariably sound in a desire for proportional representation" and "it is not even clear what fairness looks like in this context. There is a large measure of 'unfairness' in any winner-take-all system." He concluded, "Federal judges have no license to reallocate political power between the two major political parties, with no plausible grant of authority in the Constitution, and no legal standards to limit and direct their decisions."

Justice Elena Kagan, in a harsh dissent written on behalf of four justices, began by claiming, "For the first time ever, this court refuses to remedy a constitutional violation because it thinks the task beyond judicial capabilities" and "partisan gerrymanders here debased and dishonored our democracy, turning upside-down the core American idea that all governmental power derives from the people." Justice Kagan accused the court majority of ignoring these harms, of complacency, and of harboring the notion "that if we have lived with partisan gerrymanders so long, we will survive."

This ruling applies only to federal courts. During the past decade, at least ten states have invalidated legislative or commission redistricting plans because they were partisan gerrymanders or violated state redistricting criteria in an effort to draw districts that satisfied incumbents or political parties.

2011 LEGISLATIVE ENACTMENTS

Republicans dominated both the Texas House and Senate in 2011 and a Republican (Rick Perry) was governor. The legislature in regular session enacted plans for redistricting the Texas House and Senate. As might be suspected, the plans were highly partisan and gerrymandered to favor the election of Republicans. However, the legislature adjourned without enacting any plan for redrawing the state's congressional districts. Texas had been apportioned four additional seats, giving the state thirty-six congressional districts. In June 2011, a special session of the legislature enacted a congressional plan.

The decade began in a manner similar to that of previous decades, with legislative enactments, Voting Rights Act review, and court challenges to the legislative enactments. It appeared that a judicial chess match would play out as in the past. However, soon the judicial landscape in Texas was changed by *Shelby County v. Holder*.

In early 2011, the preclearance requirement of Section 5 of the Voting Rights Act was still in effect. Texas Attorney General Greg Abbott assumed (probably correctly) that the Obama DOJ would object to the state's legislative enactments. In an effort to avoid an adverse DOJ ruling, Texas chose on July 11 to file in the US District Court for the District of Columbia (*Texas v. United States*) for a declaratory judgment that the legislative enactments for the Texas House, Senate, Board of Education, and congressional districts had neither the "purpose" nor the "effect" of "denying or abridging the right to vote" of any minority protected under the act. Under Section 5 of the Voting Rights Act, the needed preclearance could be obtained either through the administrative process at the DOJ or through a declaratory judgment proceeding before a special three-judge court in the District of Columbia. Jurisdictions needing preclearance generally preferred to use the administrative process at the DOJ because it was quicker.

The DC district court denied the state's request for summary judgment and set the case for trial. The court heard the case in January 2012 and issued an opinion in August 2012, finding that, except for the State Board of Education districts, the enacted districts violated Section 5 of the VRA and denying Texas preclearance. The state's effort to gain preclearance in the DC court had failed.

While the Texas appeal was pending, the US Supreme Court decided *Shelby County v. Holder*, ruling that Section 4(b) of the Voting Rights Act, the formula used to determine which jurisdictions were subject to Section 5 preclearance, was no longer constitutional. The court vacated the DC district court's judgment denying preclearance of the legislatively enacted plans in Texas and sent the case back for further consideration in light of the *Shelby County* ruling. The DC district court dismissed the Texas case as moot in December 2013.

PEREZ V. PERRY

While the state's Section 5 preclearance case was pending before the DC District Court, the legislative enactments were challenged in federal court in Texas as violative of Section 2 of the Voting Rights Act and the Fourteenth Amendment of the US Constitution. The lawsuit challenging the senate was *Davis v. Perry*. The lawsuit challenging the House enactment was *Perez v. Perry*. The lawsuits asked that implementation of the state enactments be enjoined because they did not have the required federal preclearance since the case in DC had not yet been decided. The cases were consolidated under *Perez v. Perry* in San Antonio of the Western District of Texas.

The three-judge court consisted of District Judges Xavier Rodriguez and Orlando L. Garcia and 5th Circuit Judge Jerry Smith. In November 2011, following an evidentiary hearing in September, the court unanimously found that since the legislative enactments had not been precleared under Section 5 of the Voting Rights Act, it was necessary for the court to adopt interim plans to replace the admittedly malapportioned existing districts for the 2002 primary and general elections. The Supreme Court's *Shelby County* decision was still a year and a half in the future, so the requirement for Section 5 preclearance was still in effect. The lower court unanimously agreed on an interim state senate plan, but Judge Smith dissented with respect to the congressional and state House plans. The state requested a stay on the use of all the interim plans, which the US Supreme Court granted in December 2011.

After hearing *Perez v. Perry* in January 2012, the US Supreme Court vacated the district court's order implementing the interim plans and remanded the lawsuits for further proceedings. In the *Perez* case, the United States Supreme Court agreed that, since there was no valid legislative enactment, an interim court plan was appropriate but explained, "Section 5 prevents a state plan from being implemented if it has not been precleared. But that does not mean that the plan is of no account or that the policy judgments it reflects can be disregarded by a district court drawing an interim plan. On the contrary, the state plan serves as a starting point for the district court." This was essentially the same ruling as in *Weiser*.

In February 2012, the district court on remand ordered new interim plans for the 2012 elections. The 2012 primary and general elections were held on the basis of these plans. Thus, the 2011 legislative enactments were never used.

SETTLEMENT IN THE SENATE

In June of the following year (2013), the legislature in special session adopted the court-ordered interim senate plan as the permanent senate plan. All parties in the federal case agreed to the newly enacted legislative plan as the final remedial senate plan, and the court entered a final judgment on the senate map in September 2013.

THE LEGAL CHALLENGE TO THE STATE HOUSE AND CONGRESSIONAL DISTRICTS CONTINUES

As of 2013, the lawsuit challenging the state House and congressional districts, now *Perez v. Abbott* as Abbott had replaced Perry as governor, remained unresolved.

A new House plan and congressional plan had been enacted by the legislature at the same time in June 2013 as the new senate plan, but it did not satisfy the plaintiffs in *Perez*.

The state argued that the case should be dismissed as moot because many of the districts in the new legislative enactment were identical to the districts in the court's interim state House and congressional plans. In September 2013, the district court by a vote of 2–1 denied the state's request but concluded that a full, fair, and final review of all issues before the court could not be resolved in time for the 2014 elections. Therefore, the court ordered the 2013 legislative enactment to be used for the 2014 elections.

2014–2017 COURT ACTIVITY IN TEXAS ON THE CONGRESSIONAL AND STATE HOUSE DISTRICTS

In August 2014, the district court heard evidence in *Perez v. Perry* regarding the original legislative congressional and House plans enacted in 2011. The court held a hearing on the 2011 congressional and House enactments even though they had been replaced by new enactments in 2013. One issue before the court was whether the State of Texas had engaged in a pattern of intentional denial or abridgement of voting rights warranting reinstatement of a preclearance requirement for future Texas redistricting plans. If intentional discrimination were found, a preclearance requirement could be reinstated under Section 3 of the Voting Rights Act.

Almost three years after hearing evidence and six years after the plan was adopted by the legislature, the panel, by a vote of 2–1, with J. Smith dissenting, ruled on March 10, 2017, that the 2011 congressional map was unconstitutional and violated Section 2 of the Voting Rights Act. The majority's decision held that four districts in the plan (23, 26, 27, and 35) were unconstitutional racial gerrymanders and that the creation of congressional District 35, linking Hispanic areas in Travis and Bexar Counties, could not be justified by a need to comply with the Voting Rights Act. The panel also ruled that Texas had intentionally packed and cracked minority voters in the Dallas–Fort Worth area and in creating the configuration of District 23 in the 2011 congressional plan. However, the court rejected similar intentional vote dilution claims related to the greater Houston area.

On April 20, the same two-judge majority (J. Smith dissenting) ruled that a number of districts in the 2011 state House plan resulted in intentional vote dilution in violation of the Constitution and the Voting Rights Act. The court also found that several districts violated one-person, one-vote requirements and that one district in San Antonio had been drawn as a racial gerrymander.

The US Supreme Court later commented, "Judge Smith again dissented, on both mootness and the merits. On mootness, Judge Smith explained that, '[s]ix years later, we are still enveloped in litigation over plans that have never been used and will never be implemented.' On the merits, Judge Smith argued that the majority erroneously inferred a 'complex, widespread conspiracy of scheming and plotting, by various legislators and staff, carefully designed to obscure the alleged race-based motive, when the intent was in fact partisan.'"

The court then turned its attention to the 2013 state House and congressional enactments. It held trial on July 10–15, 2017. On August 15, 2017, the court by a vote of 2–1 (Judge Smith dissenting) ruled that, like its predecessor, the 2013 congressional plan violated the Constitution and the Voting Rights Act. Specifically, it held that congressional districts 27 and 35 violated the Constitution and the Voting Rights Act. District 27 stretched from Nueces County to Bastrop County. District 35 linked parts of Travis and Bexar Counties. This majority of the court also found that enactment of the 2013 congressional plan was intentionally discriminatory and gave the State of Texas until August 18 to advise whether it would hold a special session on redistricting to redraw the congressional plan and, in the event the state chose not to redistrict, set a remedial hearing for September 5.

On August 24, the panel by the same 2–1 majority found that the 2013 state House plan violated the Constitution and Voting Rights Act and purposefully maintained discriminatory features in the 2011 plan. The court gave the state until August 29 to indicate whether it would hold a special session of the Texas Legislature to redraw the map and set a remedial hearing for September 6 in the event the state chose not to redistrict. The state appealed to the Supreme Court and asked for a stay of the district court's announced intention to adopt remedial plans. Justice Alito temporarily stayed remedial proceedings for both the congressional and state House plans. The full Supreme Court then voted to uphold the stay and to hear the state's appeal.

On June 28, 2018, the Supreme Court in a 5–4 decision reversed the decisions of the district court except for one state House district (*Abbott v. Perez*). Earlier in 2018, the Supreme Court had summarily upheld dismissal of partisan gerrymandering claims in Texas (*Democratic Party v. Abbott* and *Morris v. Texas*). The court held there was insufficient evidence to find that the Texas Legislature had intentionally discriminated against Hispanic or African American voters. The majority opinion delivered by Justice Alito explained:

> In holding that the district court disregarded the presumption of legislative good faith and improperly reversed the burden of proof, we do not suggest either that the intent of the 2011 legislature is irrelevant or that the plans enacted in 2013 are unassailable because they were previously adopted on an interim basis by the Texas court. Rather, both the intent of the 2011 legislature and the court's adoption of the interim plans are relevant to the extent that they naturally give rise to—or tend to refute—inferences regarding the intent of the 2013 Legislature. They must be

weighed together with any other direct and circumstantial evidence of that legislature's intent. But when all the relevant evidence in the record is taken into account, it is plainly insufficient to prove that the 2013 legislature acted in bad faith and engaged in intentional discrimination. [Authorities omitted.] There is thus no need for any further prolongation of this already protracted litigation.

Only the district court's finding on House District 90 survived. The Supreme Court agreed that it was a racial gerrymander. The case was again remanded for the district court to determine what relief, if any, was appropriate in regard to District 90. Only one candidate ran in House District 90 in the 2018 general election, the incumbent Democrat Ramon Romero.

Justice Sonia Sotomayor, joined by Justices Ginsburg, Stephen Breyer, and Kagan, dissented. This dissenting opinion accused the majority of "pars[ing]" the facts to go "out of its way to permit the State of Texas to use maps that the three-judge district court unanimously found were adopted for the purpose of preserving the racial discrimination that tainted its previous maps." This reference to the "unanimous" action of a three-judge district court seems aimed at the action of the three-judge court in DC. The dissent disputed the majority's rejection of the finding on intentional discrimination and on its findings on House districts 27, 32, and 34. In 2018, Democrats won two of these three districts. All three winners were incumbents seeking reelection. In concluding, Justice Sotomayor wrote:

> The Equal Protection Clause of the Fourteenth Amendment and Section 2 of the Voting Rights Act secure for all voters in our country, regardless of race, the right to equal participation in our political processes. Those guarantees mean little, however, if courts do not remain vigilant in curbing States' efforts to undermine the ability of minority voters

to meaningfully exercise that right. For although we have made progress, voting discrimination still exists; no one doubts that.

On remand in 2018, the district court asked the parties to indicate whether they were in agreement on a remedy, if any, on House District 90. The parties remained in disagreement. The court urged the legislature to act within the first forty-five days of the regular session or the court "will proceed with a remedial phase" (*Perez v. Abbott* [Order, August 30, 2018]). On May 28, 2019, the court approved a plan that had been jointly submitted by the state and MALDEF and which resolved the dispute over House District 90.

REINSTATING A REQUIREMENT FOR PRECLEARANCE OF TEXAS REDISTRICTING PLANS

In its August 30, 2018 order, the district court also set a briefing schedule for the plaintiffs' claims under Section 3(a) of the Voting Rights Act that the State of Texas should remain under the court's jurisdiction and be placed under a preclearance requirement for any statewide redistricting plan for a term of at least five years. This claim has been part of the litigation since 2011. The plaintiffs pointed to the history of Texas redistricting as showing that the legislature had repeatedly and intentionally tried to suppress minority representation and will continue to do so unless it is required to obtain preclearance of new redistricting plans. There have been at least twenty instances in which a preclearance requirement has been imposed on a government jurisdiction. The position of the DOJ is critical in such "bail-in" lawsuits.

At one time during the Obama administration (2013), the DOJ intervened in support of the plaintiffs' claim. The

DOJ reversed its position in February 2019 under the Trump administration and now opposes any reinstatement of the preclearance requirement. This change in the DOJ's position was reportedly opposed by DOJ staff. On July 24, 2019, the district court indicated that it "found violations of the Fourteenth Amendment with regard to the 2011 plans and concludes that these findings are sufficient to trigger bail-in as a potential remedy." Despite "grave concerns," however, "the Court finds an insufficient basis upon which to award the requested bail-in relief."

2018 ELECTIONS

After the 2018 elections, Democrats made some inroads into Republicans' dominant position, but there was no "blue wave" in Texas. Republicans won all the statewide races. There were, however, significant Democratic successes in district elections.

As of 2019, there were twenty-three Republicans in the Texas delegation of thirty-six members of the US House of Representatives. There were thirteen Democrats, including two who defeated Republican incumbents in 2018. Also, important for redistricting, at least six of these elected Republicans won by less than 5 percent over their Democratic opponents. This same pattern exists in the Texas House and Senate, where Republicans remain a majority but lost seats in 2018. The chart below shows close races in 2018:

US CONGRESS

District	Incumbent in 2018	Republican Winning Percentage
7	Lizzie Pannill Fletcher (D)	-5.03%*
10	Michael McCaul (R)	4.37

21	Chip Roy (R)	2.61
22	Pete Olson (R)	4.81
23	Will Hurd (R)	.44
24	Kenny Marchant (R)	3.07
31	John Carter (R)	2.91
32	Colin Allred (D)	-5.52*

TEXAS SENATE
(only half of the senate seats were up for election in 2018)

District	Incumbent in 2018	Repulican Winning Percentage
8	Angela Paxton (R)	1.36
10	Beverly Powell (D)	-3.46*
17	Joan Huffman (R)	4.64

TEXAS HOUSE OF REPRESENTATIVES

District	Incumbent in 2018	Republican Winning Percentage
26	D. F. Miller (R)	4.82
45	Erin Zwiener (D)	-2.20*
47	Vikki Goodwin (D)	-4.80*
52	James Talarico (D)	-2.46*
65	Michelle Beckley (D)	-2.32*
66	Matt Shaheen (R)	.48
67	Jeff Leach (R)	2.30
92	Jonathan Stickland (R)	2.39
96	Bill Zedler (R)	3.63

102	Ana-Maria Ramos (D)	-5.76*
105	Thresa Meza (D)	-9.48*
108	Morgan Meyer (R)	.28
112	Angie Chen Button (R)	2.08
114	John Turner (D)	-10.30*
115	Julie Johnson (D)	-13.68*
132	Gina Calanni (D)	-.20*
135	Jon Rosenthal (D)	-3.16*
136	John Bucy III (D)	-9.64*
138	Dwayne Bohac (D)	-.10*

These districts indicate Republican losses.

An overall voting trend in the 2018 elections was demonstrated with the close race (2.6 percent difference) between incumbent Republican Senator Ted Cruz and Democratic challenger Beto O'Rourke. The Democratic strongholds were primarily in South Texas along the border with Mexico and in the urban areas of Houston, Dallas, San Antonio, Austin, Fort Worth, Beaumont–Port Arthur, and El Paso. O'Rourke carried all the counties with the state's largest cities. The Republican incumbent, Senator Ted Cruz, carried essentially the remainder of the state and won reelection. The overall vote for members of the state House of Representatives shows a pattern similar to that of the Cruz vs. O'Rourke race.

EFFECTS

Despite control of redistricting in 2011 and the Supreme Court's blockage of the most aggressive district court redistricting plans, the Republicans saw modest decreases in their numbers.

	2011	2019
Texas House of Representatives (Republicans)	101	83
Texas Senate (Republicans)	19	19
Texas Congressional Delegation (Republicans)	23 of 32	23 of 36

A majority of the members of both the senate and House remain Republican but by a smaller margin in the House than in 2011. In a special election in 2018, Pete Flores became the first Hispanic Republican elected to the Texas Senate.

In the 2010s, Republicans defended legislative enactments by asserting in court that what was being challenged as racial or ethnic discrimination was really partisan gerrymandering. Initially, this strategy looked like it would fail. A three-judge federal district court in DC found unanimously that the state's 2011 legislative enactments for congressional and state legislative districts violated Section 5 of the Voting Rights Act, but this holding was mooted and the case dismissed in light of *Shelby County*. A three-judge federal district court in San Antonio found by a vote of 2–1 that these same legislative enactments and those in 2013 were intentionally discriminatory, but these holdings were reversed by the Supreme Court in *Abbott v. Perez*. Ultimately, the United States Supreme Court made Texas Republicans the winners in most of the decade's legal battles.

CHAPTER 9

STRATEGIES FOR REDISTRICTING TEXAS IN 2021

THIS CHAPTER IS INTENDED TO provide some insight into how the legal strategists for each political group, including the political parties and minority activist organizations, are likely to see the redistricting issues in 2021.

The latest projections of the Texas Demographic Center for 2020 show a state population of approximately 30 million: 41 percent non-Hispanic white, 11.8 percent non-Hispanic black, 39.3 percent Hispanic, 5 percent non-Hispanic Asian, and 2 percent non-Hispanic other.

Republicans are likely to continue their domination of the legislative redistricting process in 2021. The Democrats' task in the 2020 election is monumental. To win a majority of the 36-member congressional delegation, Democrats must gain a net of at least six congressional seats. To win a majority of the 31-member state senate, Democrats must gain a net of at least four seats: nine seats to gain two-thirds. In either scenario, the presiding officer, Lieutenant Governor Dan Patrick, will remain Republican. To win a majority of the 150 seats in the state House, Democrats must gain at least nine net seats. If they gain a sufficient number of seats, they might be able to elect the Speaker. It is mathematically possible that Democrats could gain a majority of one or both chambers in 2020 elections, but it is unlikely.

In 2021, Republicans will hold all the offices elected state-wide likely to have an impact on redistricting, such as governor, lieutenant governor, and attorney general. All these officials were reelected in 2018 for four-year terms so, barring extraordinary events, they will remain in office throughout the redistricting process.

In terms of redistricting, this success in statewide elections gives the Republicans an advantage that could trump any Democratic success in 2020 elections. If any legislative enactment in 2021 favors Democrats, it is vulnerable to veto by the governor, Greg Abbott, who is Republican. Abbott, as attorney general, played a major role in securing passage of the congressional gerrymander in 2003. If the legislature fails to enact legislation that redistricts the state senate or House, the responsibility for redistricting that chamber passes to the Republican-controlled LRB. Even if the Speaker is a Democrat, the other four members of the LRB will remain Republican. If any redistricting enactment (other than congressional) is vetoed by Abbott, responsibility for redistricting passes to the LRB.

It is difficult to imagine how Republicans will lose in this legislative/governor/LRB process.

REPUBLICAN DOMINANCE

The Republican losses and close calls in 2018 may be reversed in 2020 or seen by some as aberrations requiring little or no reconfiguring of district boundaries to ensure Republican victories in the future. However, any Republican officeholder surviving a close election in 2018 or 2020 may wish to have a safer district by seeing the percentage of dependable Republican voters increased in his or her district during 2021 redistricting. This issue may arise in the form of a question about which election returns a political party should use to predict future voter behavior or "performance." The process can be as simple as choosing whether to give greater credence to the 2018 vote for Greg Abbott in a precinct or the vote for Senator Ted Cruz in that same precinct. For Democrats, which is the better barometer, the results for 2018 gubernatorial candidate Lupe Valdez or senatorial candidate Beto O'Rourke? There are an almost endless number of election results to consider, but which are most dependable for predicting the future? Even a blend of election results is uncertain.

Other Republicans may feel that the districts lost in 2018 or 2020 can be won back if the Republican voter percentage is increased in them. However, the number of dependably Republican voters is finite. As long as districts must be equal in population, any increase of dependably Republican voters in one district necessarily means a reduction in another district.

Democrats are unlikely to face this quandary because Republicans will still control the redistricting process and because the strategy of the Republicans is likely to be to pack as many Democrats into as few districts as possible. This strategy cedes these districts to the Democrats but causes the Democrats to waste votes by winning overwhelmingly in a few districts while losing in the majority of districts. This strategy is a classic form of gerrymandering.

Redistricting strategy for 2021 will initially turn on whether the parties are agreeable to an essentially "status quo" exercise. If so, the redistricting focus is likely to be primarily on protecting the incumbents of both parties. Incumbent protection is also likely to be a focus if Democratic and Republican strength in each chamber is roughly equal.

Some observers see retention of the status quo as the more likely strategy for both major political parties. They urge that, since the last five decades have brought a sea change in Texas politics and Republicans will probably still be a majority in the state legislature and in the congressional delegation, Republicans should adopt a policy designed to maintain this dominance for the next decade rather than to enhance it. For many reasons, it is the governor, Greg Abbott, who will be critical to determining the policy that will prevail. Democrats probably have little opportunity for any enhancement of power and thus would likely welcome such a plan. If the political parties pursue an essentially status quo result, the process will be messy as usual but minimally significant or exciting, with battles among incumbents and selective efforts to reshape the state legislative districts that Republicans or Democrats have recently won.

On the other hand, some observers think the Republican Party should seize this possibly fleeting moment of absolute dominance in the state institutions to further enhance its political position for the next decades. If so, heightened confrontation can be expected throughout the process and legal strategizing becomes important. For Republicans, this means seeing that the task of redistricting ends up in the hands of the LRB.

Under either scenario, what happens in 2021 will affect what happens in lawmaking for the next decade. The following discussion assumes at least an active consideration of aggressive policies designed to maintain and enhance political power.

THE EXPECTATION OF TWO TO THREE ADDITIONAL SEATS IN THE US HOUSE OF REPRESENTATIVES

Under Article I, Section 2, of the US Constitution, the federal government is responsible for a periodic enumeration of the persons in this country and a reapportionment of the seats in the United States House of Representatives among the states "according to their respective numbers" of persons. The census is reported to Congress at the beginning of the first year in each decade (e.g., 2021). The size of the US House was set in 1911 at 435 members. Therefore, in accordance with federal law, 2 USC Sections 2a et. seq., this number of representatives is apportioned among the states according to the "method of equal proportions" after each state is apportioned the one representative guaranteed by the US Constitution.

The census numbers, in a format that can be used for redistricting, are likely to be sent to the states in February or March 2021. In Texas, the Legislative Council will then put these numbers and associated election results in a format that can be used by members of the legislature, legislative staffs, and the public to determine populations and past voting history of any proffered plan. Texas can expect to gain two or three additional seats in Congress in 2021.

REDISTRICTING ON THE BASIS OF TOTAL POPULATION OR ELIGIBLE VOTERS (ELECTORS)

A critical question must be answered up front in 2021. The decision of the US Supreme Court in *Evenwel v. Abbott* poses the possibility that a state or its political subdivisions might redistrict on the basis of eligible voters instead of population. In many states, the differences would be small. In Texas, however, the level of racial and ethnic diversity in different parts of the state means that the differences could be great.

A use of citizen, eligible voter, or citizen voting age data rather than total population as the basis for redistricting could significantly affect African American, Asian, and Hispanic representation by reducing disproportionately the number of these persons considered for redistricting purposes. Each of the three has a high percentage of its population that is too young to qualify as voters. Both Asian and Hispanic population numbers include significant numbers of noncitizens. Hispanics in Texas could lose one or two seats in the state senate and Congress, and even more seats in the state House, if redistricting is not conducted based on total population.

ADDING A QUESTION ON CITIZENSHIP TO THE CENSUS

One of the current controversies at the national level has many potential implications for Texas. The current administration was proposing to determine whether all members of a family are citizens.

Critics claim that if an inquiry on citizenship is added to the US Census, it will reduce the number of census responses from Hispanic and Asian citizens and increase the undercount of language minorities. After a recent survey, the Census Bureau concluded, "These data suggest the question may impede participation among audiences with recent immigration history. The significance of this barrier will likely vary with individuals' beliefs about the question's purpose, their trust in the government to keep their information confidential, and beliefs about whether their ethnic group is the subject of politically motivated targeting. The barrier was highest among those individuals who believed that the purpose of the question is to find undocumented immigrants, that their information will be shared across agencies—potentially leading to deportation—and that their ethnic group is facing an inhospitable political environment." Bureau of Census staff estimated that adding the citizenship question to the census short form could cause an increased undercount of 6.5 million persons. This increase in the undercount is projected to occur among both citizens and noncitizens.

Since the apportionment of seats in Congress and the distribution of much of federal aid to states is based on a state's population, any significant undercount of these persons could reduce a state's power in Congress and share of federal money if it has a disproportionate language minority population. Ironically, Texas is among the states most likely to be affected. It has a combined Hispanic and Asian population of over 13.5 million, or approximately 45 percent of its population. The situation is ironic because it puts the state's Republican leaders in an awkward position. Politically, they support the Trump administration's effort to change the census questionnaire and do not worry about undercounting Hispanic and Asian persons, since these persons "are probably Democrats anyway." On the other hand, any undercount of these persons is likely to harm the state. As a result, these Republican officials, who frequently intervened in lawsuits to challenge federal policies under the Obama administration, have said little or nothing about the proposed census change.

In a decision (*Dept. of Commerce v. New York*) on June 27, 2019, the Supreme Court ruled by 5–4 that the census would go forward without the question on citizenship. Three US district courts found that the process by which the question was approved for addition to the census violated the federal Administrative Procedures Act and enjoined addition of the question. In an opinion written by Chief Justice Roberts, the court found that the rationale offered by the government for including the citizenship question "seems to have been contrived." However, President Trump insisted that the DOJ come up with an acceptable rationale and go back to ask the court to change its ruling. He later gave up on this idea and announced that he would order federal agencies to cooperate in comingling lists to provide the number of noncitizens. Whether such a count of noncitizens is viable in this manner is unclear. Even if such a combined list is achieved, it is unlikely to have the credibility or specificity of the census or the accuracy to permit redistricting on the basis of citizens.

More recently, President Trump has announced his intention to deduct the number of undocumented immigrants from each state's total population before forwarding the census numbers to the Congress for the purpose of apportioning congressional seats. It is uncertain whether this outcome will occur or even if it will be feasible. If it does occur, it will probably reduce the number of congressional seats assigned to Texas.

REDISTRICTING ON THE BASIS OF THE NUMBER OF CITIZENS (ELIGIBLE VOTERS)

The US is known for using total population from the decennial census as the basis for redistricting. Some other nations use either number of citizens or number of eligible voters.

Data for redistricting in the US comes from a reliable, unbiased census available at the block and precinct levels. Currently, any calculation of citizens or citizens of voting age in an area requires inference from data now available only at the much larger census block group level. Such inferences are often unreliable. This means that in the past, using citizenship for redistricting has been unacceptable.

Those in favor of requiring total population to be equalized among electoral districts emphasize that every inhabitant is entitled to equal representation and that noncitizens and the young have legitimate issues as well. Proponents of using population point to the history of the usage of total population for redistricting in the US and the initial decision of the members of the Constitutional Convention in 1787 and the authors of the Fourteenth Amendment to use total population as the basis for apportioning seats in Congress. Writing for the court in *Evenwel*, Justice Ginsburg explained:

As the Framers of the Constitution and the Fourteenth Amendment comprehended, representatives serve all residents, not just those eligible or registered to vote.

Nonvoters have an important stake in many policy debates—children, their parents, even their grandparents, for example, have a stake in a strong public-education system—and in receiving constituent services, such as help in navigating public-benefits bureaucracies. By ensuring that each representative is subject to requests and suggestions from the same number of constituents, total population apportionment promotes equitable and effective representation.

Areas inhabited primarily by noncitizens or the young have needs, such as health care and housing. Should these areas be entitled to equal representation?

Opponents of using total population as the basis for drawing districts point to several drawbacks. Primarily, they argue that a noncitizen or someone too young to vote has no right to affect who makes US policy. Proponents of a change from population to a voter-eligible metric also point to the fact that most countries worldwide redistrict using citizen population or eligible voters and to the enormous disparity in Texas among the existing districts between the number of qualified voters and turned-out voters on the one hand and total population on the other hand. For example, among Texas congressional districts:

	District 21	District 29
Population (2010 census)	698,488	698,488
Registered Voters (2016)	542,873	270,160
Vote (2016)	365,284	133,965

They also point out that census data may be inaccurate. In 2010, it was estimated that the US Census undercount was about 1.6 percent, with a higher percentage for certain minorities. Decennial census data also becomes obsolete. Districts drawn on the basis of a periodic census become malapportioned as the population changes or shifts during that period. It may be financially or practically infeasible to conduct a national census more often than once per decade; therefore, a reliable census may be unavailable later in a decade. Of course, obtaining citizenship data through the decennial census would have these same problems, or even more, if critics are right that some Asian and Hispanic persons would avoid answering the census even though they are citizens.

IS THE USE OF CITIZEN DATA LEGAL FOR TEXAS REDISTRICTING?

Any attempt to base redistricting on citizen, eligible voter, or citizen voting age data instead of population is certain to be challenged in state or federal court. In view of the suggestion in *Evenwel* that as a general matter either base is acceptable, the success of the challenges will depend on the circumstances and applicable law. However, the ruling in *Dept. of Commerce v. New York* that a question on citizenship may not appear on the basic census questionnaire leaves the issue of citizenship for an area to be determined by inference, which is necessarily less dependable and more legally vulnerable than actual enumeration on the census. President Trump's plans for interagency cooperation seem to change little and have ample room for error.

The American Community Survey (ACS) now estimates certain characteristics over time, including citizenship, in an area. Only approximately three million addresses are surveyed each year. The data are pooled to produce five-year reports. Although a valuable tool, ACS estimates are ill-suited for redistricting.

The fundamental challenge in Texas to any change from population will likely be under Section 2 of the Voting Rights Act and the state and federal constitution on the basis that a change to counting only citizens would unlawfully discriminate against Asians and Hispanics. Certainly, such a change would have an adverse effect on these groups and reduce the number of electoral districts in Texas with Hispanic majorities. The legality otherwise of such a change also depends on the wording of the specific constitutional provisions applicable to each type of district.

In regard to congressional districts, there is no provision of the US or Texas constitutions that requires that members of Congress be elected from districts, much less that declares expressly whether those districts should be drawn on the basis of citizens or population. (Nor does the Texas Constitution impose any requirement that the fifteen members of the State Board of Education be elected, much less that they be elected from districts of equal population.) The requirement for single-member congressional districts is in a federal statute, not the Constitution. However, many federal cases have spoken in the past about "population" as the basis for redistricting congressional districts within a state. Article I, Section 2, of the US Constitution requires that seats in the House of Representatives be apportioned among the states "according to their respective numbers": that is, population.

This wording may indirectly require that congressional electoral districts be drawn on the basis of population, because it would seem strange that the founders of this country required apportionment based on population but envisioned that a state could use citizenship for drawing electoral districts. Moreover, the guarantee of equal protection under the Fourteenth Amendment of the United States

Constitution applies to each person rather than to each citizen. It must be noted that at least two nations (Canada and Australia) apportion seats in their national parliament on the basis of population but permit or require provinces to draw electoral districts using citizenship data.

As regards the Texas House of Representatives, the Texas Constitution is clearer. Article III, Section 26, requires the apportionment of the members of the Texas House of Representatives on the basis of the "population" of each county "on a ratio obtained by dividing the population of the State, as ascertained by the most recent United States census" by the number of members in the Texas House of Representatives. There would appear to be little or no room under this provision to use any base other than total population as shown by the federal census.

The Texas Senate was directly at issue in *Evenwel*. The case makes clear that population may be used to draw electoral districts. Census population has been consistently used in the past and the legislature would be wise to continue to do so. Article III, Section 25, was amended in 2001 and now has no explicit base for drawing districts. As adopted in 1876, the section provided that the senate districts were to be drawn using "qualified electors."

However, this distinction may be rooted in discrimination. It appears that this "elector" wording originated in earlier constitutions at a time when neither blacks nor women could vote and, although counted in the enumeration, were not electors. Section 25 was declared unconstitutional in *Kilgarlin v. Martin*, but it may be argued that the ruling applied at the time only to the section's limit of one senator per county, not to its reference to "electors." Republicans raised this issue in state court litigation in 1981.

For many reasons, it would be unwise for the Texas Legislature to redraw any of these electoral districts on the basis of citizen, eligible voter, or CVAP data. This issue will be raised, but the argument for abandoning the use of total population figures in redistricting is unlikely to prevail in 2021. However, in view of the nationwide controversy about the number and role of undocumented immigrants, it is likely that some part of the Republican Party will want to draw congressional, state senate, state Board of Education, or state House of Representatives districts using something other than population.

It is in local governments in which the use of citizen data for redistricting may first appear in 2021, as some county, city, or school board sees a change from population as politically beneficial.

REPUBLICAN STRATEGY FOR 2021

Assuming an aggressive Republican strategy, I believe the following issues will arise.

Although it is very unlikely that the 2020 election will threaten the dominance of Republicans over redistricting, it might bring changes in Washington, DC, that will affect Texas. If a Democrat wins the presidency, the DOJ's attitude toward Texas redistricting will be less favorable than it was under Trump. Even if the VRA Section 5 preclearance requirement is gone, there are many ways in which this change at the DOJ might affect Texas voters. For example, the DOJ could re-reverse its position about whether to reinstate the preclearance requirement for Texas redistricting plans. Much of the legal action in 2021 is likely to focus on this possibility.

Potential Democratic control of the US Senate could make a difference in legislation enacted by Congress, including for redistricting.

DRAW STATE LEGISLATIVE DISTRICTS IN THE LRB

The LRB has drawn all or part of the state's legislative districts in three of the past five decades. History has shown that the LRB can draw highly partisan state legislative plans and that it can be a stepping-stone for political success.

The LRB in 2021 will probably consist of Dan Patrick, Ken Paxton, George P. Bush, Glenn Hegar, and a to-be-determined Speaker of the House. All are Republican or likely will be. Some of these officials can be expected to have their eyes on higher office. The LRB can provide a valuable political platform. Being the architect of a strongly Republican partisan redistricting plan may be a way of proving LRB members' partisan credentials and influencing their voter base.

Still irritated by the century or more that it took Republicans to regain control of those houses of the state legislature, the Republican Party (or the LRB) is unlikely to accept anything but a partisan plan that is designed to give the party a safe majority in the House of Representatives and possibly a clear 20 to 22 member majority in the senate. Even if the lieutenant governor and Speaker publicly favor a status quo plan to protect their members, they cannot necessarily control the outcome. In 2001, Speaker Pete Laney (Democrat) and Lieutenant Governor Bill Ratliff (Republican) both wanted incumbent-friendly (status quo) plans but could not get such a plan through the legislature or the LRB.

Some members of the LRB will have allies in the legislature who favor having the LRB redistrict. If some Republican legislators resolve to send redistricting to the LRB, it may be relatively simple, even with some Republican dissenters, to block any legislative enactment, thereby leaving the task of state legislative redistricting to the LRB. If the legislators demure, the governor may veto the legislative enactments and send the matter to the LRB.

The LRB option may become widely attractive to Republicans if the Democrats make further inroads into the Republican legislative majorities in the 2020 elections. Why bother with the partisan battles of a divided legislature when all redistricting of legislative districts can be done by five Republican officials?

TAKE ADVANTAGE OF NO VOTING RIGHTS ACT PRECLEARANCE REVIEW

The ruling in *Shelby County* effectively ended VRA Section 5 preclearance review of Texas redistricting plans. The redistricting in 2021 will be the first time since 1971 in which plans enacted by the legislature can take effect without first obtaining federal approval. This does not include the occasions when the legislature allowed plans drawn by federal courts to remain in effect. Will Republicans take advantage of the absence of the required DOJ review to adopt plans that could be interpreted as adversely affecting minorities?

The elongated predominantly Hispanic congressional and state senate districts in South Texas might appear as an opportunity for replacing these districts with more compact ones. Such a change would encounter many legal problems. Two of the existing congressional districts (15 and 27) in South Texas owe their basic shape to the federal court in *Upham* from 1981. The districts were drawn in place of two more compact districts to purposefully combine the border counties (Hidalgo and Cameron), which have an extremely high percentage of Hispanic population, with counties further north that have lower percentages of Hispanic population, to form two districts with a majority of Hispanic voters in which Hispanics could still elect the person of their choice. The compact district effectively packed Hispanics into one district. These districts, along with Congressional District 28, were given further court blessings over the years. Any attempt in 2021 to alter their basic shape to draw more compact, but fewer "opportunity to elect," Hispanic districts would likely be in violation of Section 2 of the Voting Rights Act.

There are other minority districts that can become targets, especially in and near Dallas and Harris Counties, now that Section 5 is no longer in effect. Since Colin Allred is African American, Congressional District 32 may have VRA protection. Moreover, Section 2 of the Voting Rights Act has proven to be a potent weapon in the hands of skilled, mostly Hispanic and African American attorneys.

Several jurisdictions, including at least one in Texas, have had the preclearance requirement reinstated by a federal court under Section 3(a) of the Voting Rights Act. The federal court in *Perez v. Abbott* decided against doing so for Texas redistricting plans but cautioned that it had "grave concerns." This court found violations of the Fourteenth Amendment that could be a starting point for any future analysis. Texas must be cautious in its future redistricting and must not enact plans that infringe on minority rights. As the court concluded, "Given the fact of changing population demographics, the likelihood increases that the Texas Legislature will continue to find ways to attempt to engage in 'ingenious defiance of the Constitution' that necessitated the preclearance system in the first place."

It is unwise for Republicans to rely on the US Supreme Court to reject a finding that this state has engaged in a pattern of intentional discrimination, especially if a Democrat wins the presidency in 2020 and a future DOJ supports such a finding.

UNDERPOPULATE DISTRICTS THAT ARE EXPECTED TO GROW—NOT MINORITY DISTRICTS

Historically, Texas has underpopulated, within the 10 percent standard, many of the state legislative districts with African American or Hispanic majorities. This was done in the past because of the recognition of the disproportional undercount of these categories of persons that usually occurs in the federal census. An effect of the underpopulation of these minority districts, however, was theoretically to allow more minority and Democratic voters in other districts.

At the same time, some Republicans have urged the underpopulation of strongly Republican districts that are expected to disproportionately increase in population during the next decade. This latter policy would theoretically allow more Republican voters to be spread among other districts. Of course, this assumption may change if Democrats continue to make inroads in these fast-growing "bedroom" communities or if the likely Democratic districts (e.g., Houston, Austin, South Texas, etc.) are among the fastest growing. Also, the rapid growth of population in some counties may depend on ever-changing economic conditions (e.g., the oil and gas boom in Midland, Ector, and Gaines Counties) that will not necessarily be repeated in the next decade.

Either policy for the systematic underpopulation of certain districts to enhance the strength of a political group must be pursued cautiously (if at all) in view of the state's burdens explained in *Larios v. Cox*. As discussed above, though, the lack of DOJ preclearance gives any Republican majority more latitude.

CAPTURE THE NEW CONGRESSIONAL SEATS

Texas was estimated by the Census Bureau to have 27,469,114 residents by July 1, 2015 (a gain of approximately 2,323,009 persons from the previous count). This rate of growth is 9.2 percent compared to a national average of 4.1 percent. If this growth continues, Texas is likely to be apportioned two or three new congressional seats in 2021. Some of the portions of the state, especially the urban counties and counties bordering the urban counties, have experienced disproportionately high population growth during the past decade. Harris County alone is estimated to have grown by 444,952 persons in the first five years of this decade.

The existing congressional districts covering these areas are overpopulated. Republicans in the past have argued that most of the new congressional districts apportioned to Texas should be drawn to encompass these areas rather than fast-growing South Texas. The counties in South Texas are not among the fastest growing thus far this decade. Any congressional redistricting plan passed by Republican majorities in the House of Representatives and senate is likely to try to draw the majority of any new congressional districts so that they are likely to elect a Republican in 2021.

SHORE UP THE DISTRICTS OF INCUMBENT REPUBLICANS

The downside for Republicans of having a majority in congressional, state House, and state senate seats is that there are now many more Republican incumbents who want their districts changed to add reliable Republican voters, especially given the closer-than-expected races in 2018, and the Republicans who lost in districts once thought to be safely Republican. However, there are only a finite number of voters who can be assumed to always vote for Republicans. Many more lean Republican but may occasionally vote for a Democrat.

Drawing politically "safe" districts is a risky zero-sum game. Spreading staunch Republican voters among too many districts means that, under changed circumstances, many Republican legislators could be swept from office, especially since some Republican incumbents had narrower-than-expected victories in 2018. Further, those incumbents are aware that several of their members who held districts once thought to be safely Republican lost to Democratic challengers in 2018. On the other hand, any decision to hoard these dependable voters to fashion "safe" districts for only a few Republicans means leaving other incumbents and the Party's majority vulnerable. Also, for two of the reelected Republican congressmen (Districts 23 and 27), any reduction in minority percentage raises a potential problem under the Voting Rights Act. Republicans face a dilemma, but one that is certainly preferable to the one faced by Democrats.

FIND AN ACCEPTABLE WAY TO DEAL WITH POPULATION LOSS IN THE RURAL DISTRICTS AND THE DECLINING PERCENTAGE OF NON-HISPANIC WHITES STATEWIDE

The rural areas of Texas generally grew less in population than the state on average. At least ninety-nine of Texas's 254 counties are projected to lose population over the next thirty years. Among the counties losing population most rapidly are Castro, Clay, Comanche, Floyd, Hale, Jeff Davis, Lamb, Parmer, Presidio, and Sabine. These counties are projected to lose from 34 to 66 percent of their population over this period. As a result, these areas will lose representation, especially in the Texas House of Representatives. The rural representatives are mostly Republican, so it is almost certain that six or more Republican incumbents from rural Texas will end up paired in the Texas House districts.

Related questions arise concerning whether and where to count convicted felons confined in state prisons. Texas has the largest prison population in the nation, with over 142,000 inmates. These convicted felons cannot vote but are counted in the census in the county where confined. This is a seemingly small number of inhabitants in a state of over 25 million, but these prisoners are primarily concentrated in facilities in fifty-eight mostly rural counties. For example, over 23 percent of the census population in Anderson County is in prisons located in the county. Other counties, such as Jones, Karnes, Madison, and Walker, have similar but slightly smaller percentages.

Many of these counties exclude inmates from their redistricting of county commissioner precincts because otherwise a precinct containing the prison might have very few eligible voters and be significantly unequal in voters from the other three precincts. On the other hand, the state has not historically adjusted this population used for state redistricting. As a result, legislative districts, especially in the House, that contain one or more counties with these prisons may appear equal in population with other districts but be significantly lower in number of qualified voters.

A new wrinkle has been added. Most of the inmates in rural prisons were residing in urban counties when arrested and convicted. The Bureau of Census has offered to allocate these inmates to the county in which they resided before arrest rather than to the county of confinement. If Texas takes advantage of this change, the census population would further shift from rural to urban counties. Republicans stand to lose representation if this change is made.

The Republican Party for at least sixty years has been a party dominated by non-Hispanic whites. As the political power of the Republican Party has grown, however, its base of non-Hispanic white voters has shrunk. In 2000, this category of Texan constituted 52.4 percent of the state's population. By 2010, the percentage had dropped to 45.3 percent. Projections show that by 2020, non-Hispanic whites, at 41.9 percent, will remain the largest single component of the state's population, but only barely.

DEFEAT NEW DEMOCRATIC INCUMBENTS

Democrats defeated several Republican incumbents in 2018. They may win more in 2020. As newcomers, these Democrats may be vulnerable in future elections. Some Republicans may feel that the addition to these districts of a few more dependably Republican voters would allow Republicans to regain these seats. Essentially, this is another competing need for the finite cache of dependable Republican voters.

DEMOCRATIC STRATEGY FOR 2021

As a general matter, Democrats can be expected to assume a defensive posture on redistricting in 2021 or risk making true the statement lobbed at them by Tom DeLay in Congress in 2003: "They are irrelevant."

DEMOCRATIC DISADVANTAGES

Democrats have lost several advantages that they had last decade. On the federal level, Barack Obama is no longer president and preclearance review is gone. This means that the DOJ is no longer necessarily a friend in election disputes. The outcome of the 2020 election will not bring back VRA Section 5, but it could make the DOJ friendlier to minority interests.

Perhaps more important, the state and federal court systems are less welcoming to litigation that challenges state action. The possibility of challenging political gerrymandering in federal court is gone. Neither the Supreme Court of the US nor the Supreme Court of Texas appears eager to overturn a Republican redistricting plan unless it clearly evidences racial or ethnic discrimination. Even this possibility may be a thing of the past. In many US Supreme Court decisions, it was Justice Kennedy who provided the fifth vote and wrote the court opinions in redistricting cases. He has retired. Brett Kavanaugh is in. Will Chief Justice Roberts assume Justice Kennedy's role?

The bottom line is that the Democratic and minority group leaders may have to depend more on their political wiles than on their lawyers.

REMEMBER THE LRB AND 2001

The LRB will be composed of at least four Republicans. If it gets the opportunity to redraw the legislative districts, its plan will be extremely favorable to Republicans, as it was in 2001. An LRB plan is unlikely to be successfully challenged in court. There will not be any preclearance review by the DOJ. Moreover, only the most blatant discrimination against racial or ethnic minorities is likely to be invalidated by the US Supreme Court or the Texas Supreme Court.

Democrats must find a way to avoid redistricting by the LRB, including the possibility of accepting a less than desirable legislative enactment. If this fails, then the focus must be on reinstatement of preclearance under VRA Section 3(a).

INCREASING OVERALL DEMOCRATIC STRENGTH BY REDUCING THE PERCENTAGE OF AFRICAN AMERICANS IN SOME DISTRICTS

Much of the Democratic voting strength statewide is concentrated in urban districts that are heavily African American and vote overwhelmingly for Democratic candidates. Many Democratic leaders feel that these districts contain a much larger percentage of African American voters than is necessary to ensure that the districts remain ones in which African American voters can elect the person of their choice. They argue that by packing African American voters in these districts, the overall political strength of both African Americans and Democrats is wasted.

In 2018, many heavily African American districts voted 80 to 90 percent for the Democrat. In 2001, Democrats presented redistricting plans that, if adopted, would have shifted some of this African American population into other districts, thus increasing the dependable Democratic vote in those other districts. None of these plans won legislative or LRB approval.

African Americans, both voters and officeholders, differ in their opinion about the wisdom of such a shift. On the one hand, African American voters now register and vote in percentages that are generally equivalent to or higher than non-Hispanic whites in nearby areas. Moreover, given their tendency to vote as a bloc, African American voters can theoretically control the outcome in the Democratic primary and then general election in a predominantly Democratic district with less than a majority of the population of the district.

By 2019, there were six African Americans in the state's congressional delegation, including one Republican. All six of these members of Congress were elected in districts that lacked an African American majority. So long as African Americans turn out in significant numbers and vote heavily Democratic, there is considerable pent-up Democratic potential in these heavily African American districts that could be spread among other districts and make those districts Democratic or competitive.

Nevertheless, any significant reduction of African American voting strength in a district creates some risk that the district is less "safe" for African Americans' preferred candidates. Some people see any reduction of the African American percentage of voters in a district as a return to earlier times, when the election of an African American was readily sacrificed for the success of non-Hispanic white Democrats. Others counter that this shift could be made on a district-by-district basis without endangering the election of African American candidates and that African American voters overall would benefit by the increased number of Democrats (regardless of race or ethnicity) elected to the legislative body.

In 2003, Republicans tried to win African American support for their congressional redistricting plan to defeat Democratic incumbents by including in their plan a new district with an African American majority. African American legislators were split. One of the African American House members was openly for the Republican proposal, but as one of the Democratic African American senators explained to me, "I can count. . . . It is more important to have the votes for what I feel is important than to have one more person at the table that looks like me." The speaker was State Senator Rodney Ellis.

AFRICAN AMERICAN VOTERS

African American voters are concentrated within the core areas of most populous counties. This concentration makes it technically easy to draw districts that give African Americans the opportunity to elect a person of their choice but also easy to pack them into overwhelmingly African American districts that effectively waste their overall influence.

Most of the existing districts represented by Democratic African Americans in the Texas House, Texas Senate, and in Congress from Texas are districts protected by the Voting Rights Act. They are therefore largely immune from any significant change that endangers their ability to elect the person of their choice, except as necessary to balance population. There is one Republican African American in the congressional delegation. For the first time since 1899, there is a Republican African American in the Texas House of Representatives.

Unlike the growing population of Hispanic and Asian voters in Texas, the statewide percentage of African American population has remained and is projected to remain relatively stable at 11 to 13 percent. Its representation in the Texas Legislature too has remained steady at around fourteen to nineteen members since 1981. The possibility of a future increase in this number may depend on the decision of African American leaders about the possibility of decreasing the percentage of African American voters in the districts that are overwhelmingly African American by moving a portion of these voters to nearby districts that have elected non-Hispanic white state representatives or senators in the past. Some African Americans see this as a wise political strategy for the future, but others see it as a step backward, potentially endangering past political gains.

HISPANIC ORGANIZATIONS

An initial concern for Hispanics is to maintain total population—not the number of citizens, eligible voters, or CVAP—as the basis for redistricting. Although not obvious, there is a difference between these categories, and there are examples worldwide of nations that use each of these different categories for redistricting. An "eligible voter" base can mean only those persons that have registered as voters. A "citizen" base includes citizen children too young to vote but excludes recent immigrants and other noncitizens. A "citizen voting age population (CVAP)" base includes only citizens old enough to vote (i.e., over age 18). As mentioned earlier, while it is doubtful that the legislature would discard total population, there are Republicans who favor such a change.

For the past three decades, various Hispanic organizations have urged the creation of a number of districts with Hispanic voting majorities proportional to the percentage of Hispanic total population in the state. As support for this objective, the organizations have pointed to the state's historic discrimination against Hispanics, the rapid growth of the Hispanic population in Texas in proportion to other racial or ethnic groups, and the decline statewide of the percentage of non-Hispanic white residents. Almost 60 percent of the population growth in Texas during the 1990s was Hispanic. These organizations have been very successful in enhancing Hispanic voting strength but have never achieved this goal of "proportional representation."

Several circumstances adversely affect any attempt to reach proportional representation for Hispanics in Texas through the drawing of legislative districts with a majority of Hispanic voters. First, unlike African Americans, who remain largely concentrated in contiguous census areas within the urban counties, Hispanics are more dispersed around the state and even within the counties themselves. The 2010 census showed some dispersion to surrounding suburbs.

Second, the percentage of Hispanics in Texas counties varies enormously. For instance, counties such as Archer, Clay, and Montague are around 15 percent Hispanic, whereas Cameron, Hidalgo, and Webb are 80 to 90 percent Hispanic. Compact congressional or state senate districts encompassing only or primarily these latter counties are similarly high in their percentage of Hispanics. From the standpoint of most Hispanic organizations, the effect of such compact districts is to pack and to waste Hispanic votes. For this reason, these organizations have favored creation of the less compact districts that stretch from the southern border of Texas to less heavily Hispanic areas of Central Texas.

Third and most important as a factor in the drawing of a district meant to allow Hispanics to elect the person of their choice is the disproportionately high ineligibility of Hispanics to register and vote. About half of the Hispanic population in Dallas and Harris Counties is ineligible to vote due to a higher percentage of noncitizens there than among the population as a whole and of a lower median age of the Hispanic population such that a larger percentage is too young to register and vote. Thus, for a district to have a majority Hispanic voting population, 70 to 75 percent of the total population must be Hispanic. Moreover, as shown by local government litigation over the past two decades, this great disparity between the percentages of Hispanic population and citizen voting age population can make it difficult for Hispanic plaintiffs to meet the requirements of *Gingles* for stating a claim under the Voting Rights Act. As previously noted, the US Supreme Court in *Thornburg v. Gingles* (1986) established three essential prongs that a group must show to get relief under Section 2 of the Voting Rights Act. These are: (1) the group is sufficiently large and compact to constitute a majority of eligible voters in a single-member district, (2) the group is politically cohesive, and (3) a white majority usually votes as a bloc to defeat candidates favored by the group.

A fourth factor will affect measures in 2021. The heavily Hispanic counties in South Texas are not estimated to have been among the fastest growing counties over the past decade. This change from recent decades makes it more difficult to argue that one or more of the new congressional districts should be placed in this area and to draw such a district.

It is reasonable to expect that Hispanic organizations will continue in 2021 to seek adoption of districts by the legislature, LRB, or courts that maximize the number of districts containing a majority Hispanic voting age population. Given that Texas is expected to be apportioned two or three additional congressional seats, these organizations will probably try to achieve an outcome in which at least two of these districts provide Hispanic voters with an opportunity to elect the person of their choice. Eyes will be focused on the number and distribution of Hispanics in the Dallas–Fort Worth area to see whether the census shows a Hispanic community large and compact enough to constitute a legal duty to create a majority Hispanic voter congressional or senate district in the area.

Among the lingering issues that have retarded Hispanic voting strength since Texas first won its independence is the low percentage of registration and turnout among eligible Hispanic voters. There are many reasons suggested as to why such issues have proven so intractable. Even the presence of statewide Hispanic candidates has failed to generate the wave of Hispanic voters that Democrats have sought. For example, fewer than half of the Hispanics in Texas are registered to vote; that equates to only 30 percent of the registered voters in the state. This is far below the rate of registration among Anglos and African Americans. Low voter turnout statewide has been a chronic problem. Texas is last in the nation in overall turnout—mostly because of the low turnout among Hispanics. Some writers are predicting, however, that Hispanic voter turnout is increasing (as shown by the 2018 mid-term elections) and could turn the state blue in 2020. Democrats have made similar predictions in the past, but none have proven true.

A new issue for Hispanics in 2021 is the extent to which they remain politically cohesive. Two incumbent Hispanic Democratic congressmen have been defeated by Republicans in districts drawn with a Hispanic majority. These seats (congressional districts 23 and 27) remained in Republican hands in 2018. Were these outcomes primarily a result of strong Hispanic support for the Republican candidates, thus raising the question of cohesion among Hispanic voters, or a polarized vote from the non-Hispanic white voters in the districts? Election experts will be offering opinions on this question during the legislative session and possibly later in court. It is clear, however, that some Republican statewide candidates, such as Abbott, attract a large share of Hispanic votes. None of these state officials will be on the 2020 ballot.

An additional development was the victory of Republican Pete Flores over Democrat Pete Gallego in a San Antonio special election for a state senate seat. The election was held to fill the remaining term of disgraced former state senator Carlos Uresti, who resigned his seat after being convicted in federal court of eleven felony charges. Flores's win marks the first time a Hispanic Republican has been elected to the Texas Senate.

In summary, my prediction: Republicans will retain control of the redistricting process in 2021.

CHAPTER 10

UNDOING

GERRYMANDERING

TEXAS REDISTRICTING OVER THE PAST 150 years provides many lessons. The question is whether Texans have learned those lessons. The single most consequential aspect of Texas politics in the past and for the foreseeable future is the state's diversity. Redistricting in Texas is complicated because this state has a substantial geographic, racial, ethnic, and electoral diversity. Even within a political party, political interests vary greatly among different racial and ethnic cultures and between rural and urban areas in different parts of the state.

In the early nineteenth century, there were four main "minority" cultures. Once dominant, the Native Americans are essentially gone. Native Americans currently constitute less than .5 percent of the Texas population. For the past seventy years, African Americans have comprised a steady 10 to 15 percent of the state's population. Hispanics were a small percentage of the state's resident population in the mid-nineteenth century but have consistently increased in numbers. For many years, a significant number of Hispanics moved freely over the border with Mexico and essentially resided part of the time in both countries. Today they constitute over 39 percent of the state's population and are predicted to become a majority by the middle of this century. Asian Americans are a meaningful addition to the state's diverse population, with a growing cohort of approximately 5 percent of the population.

Together, these "minority" cultures make up over half of the state's population. Anglos have been a majority of the state's population for almost two centuries, but now non-Hispanic whites make up only about 41 percent. This percentage is declining. They remain a majority, however, of the state's qualified voters. This too is likely to end.

Thus, neither political party is likely to win elections in the future by relying solely on the vote of one group. These demographic evolutions are predicted to continue. The Texas Demographic Center projects the following changes:

Group	2000 Census	2010 Census	2020	2030	2050
White	10,933,313	11,397,345	12,138,523	12,774,056	13,523,839
Black	2,364,255	2,886,835	3,557,892	4,322,983	6,030,795
Asian	554,445	948,426	1,525,629	2,414,732	5,782,908
Hispanic	6,669,666	9,460,921	11,804,659	14,452,949	20,191,750
Other	330,141	452,044	651,069	929,709	1,813,125

The numbers for 2020–2050 are only projections, so the real demographics may differ, but according to these projections, Hispanics will constitute the largest group in the state's population at some point in the 2020s and a near majority of the state's population by 2050. The non-Hispanic white or Anglo percentage of the population will decline to approximately 28.5 percent by 2050.

It is a mistake, however, to assume that any racial or ethnic group of voters is necessarily cohesive or that, even if cohesive, the group will always support the candidates of a particular political party. African American voters now consistently vote Democratic, but there was a time when they voted overwhelmingly for Republican candidates. The first African American Republican congressman in modern times from Texas, Will Hurd, was elected in 2016 and reelected in 2018; Hurd will be retiring at the end of his term. Similarly, the first African American Republican in the Texas House in the past 100 years, James White, is now serving and won reelection in 2018. Are these aberrations, or something more?

Hispanic Republicans also have had some success in Texas. One of the US senators, Ted Cruz, is Hispanic, as is one of the state's Republican congressmen, Bill Flores. The first Hispanic Republican in modern times, Pete Flores, won election to the current state senate. There were three Hispanic Republicans in the House, but two lost their bids for reelection in 2018 in the Republican primary. A majority of Hispanic voters continues to vote for Democrats, but a significant percentage has supported Republican candidates such as Greg Abbott and George W. Bush. At least one poll claims to show that Hispanic voters generally preferred Abbott over his Democratic Hispanic opponent in the 2018 gubernatorial election. On the other hand, Democratic non-Hispanic white candidate Beto O'Rourke consistently won more votes in heavily Hispanic counties than his opponent Ted Cruz. One poll suggests that O'Rourke received approximately 64 percent of the Hispanic vote.

There was a time in Texas history when an overwhelming majority of Anglo voters supported Democratic candidates. In recent elections in Texas, an overwhelming majority has consistently voted Republican, but in 2018, Democratic non-Hispanic candidates won at least twelve seats from Republicans in the Texas House, Senate, and US congressional elections.

When Texas was founded, women were neither able to vote nor even counted for purposes of redistricting. Once the US census replaced the state enumeration, women were at least included as persons to be counted. Women were recognized as citizens in the State Constitution of 1869 but did not have the right to vote until ratification of the 19th Amendment to the US Constitution in 1920. The Texas Legislature consists mostly of men. The 86th Legislature in 2019 had thirty-three women out of 181 members. The peak number of women was thirty-seven in 2009.

REMEDYING PAST RACIAL AND ETHNIC DISCRIMINATION

Much of the ethnic diversity in Texas has its foundation in the state's history and geography. South Texas was once solidly Hispanic and a target of discrimination through malapportionment and neglect in the redistricting process. The courts, through a requirement for population equality and the Voting Rights Act, partially remedied that discrimination, but Hispanics have had to fight in court for four decades to avoid further discrimination. Now South Texas is once again becoming more and more Hispanic, but Hispanic activist groups no longer have Section 5 of the Voting Rights Act as a means of preventing legislative malfeasance. Will Hispanics again become the target of discrimination through districts that are compact but have a packing effect?

African Americans were effectively shut out of the political process in Texas until the door was first cracked in the 1970s. Now, they face the dilemma of whether to fight to keep African American percentages high in a few districts to guarantee that those districts are "safe" for African American and Democratic candidates or to see some of the African American and Democratic voters included in other districts to make those other districts more competitive. Recent victories by African Americans in districts lacking an African American majority are a positive sign.

Many of the interests of the two largest minority groups, African American and Hispanic, differ. As a rule, these two groups are not electorally cohesive except possibly in general election contests. Merely because a majority of both of these minority groups currently tends to support Democratic candidates in general elections does not mean that the interests of the political party are coterminous with or take priority over the interests of these voters, especially in the redistricting process. Conflicts abound. In some instances, the electoral success of African Americans in a district is due in part to the low voter registration and turnout of Hispanics within that district, especially in the Democratic primary. It is inaccurate for anyone to assume that the organizations representing these minority groups are merely proxies for the Democratic Party.

RECOGNIZING THE IMPORTANCE OF "ONE PERSON, ONE VOTE"

Gerrymanders in Texas are neither new nor as harmful as sometimes portrayed. I am not an apologist for partisan gerrymandering, but I think its effectiveness is overrated. For thirty-five years I have fought for the use of partisan-neutral, legitimate factors in redistricting through the application of legal standards and criteria to the process. Legal standards set the parameters of what is allowable. I have learned, however, that they are not enough to control what occurs within those parameters. Moreover, I have become skeptical of finding any effective means of restraining the tendency of politicians to succumb to personal and partisan interests within these legal parameters. The only solution is to take politicians out of the redistricting process.

Some are successful; some are not. The gerrymandering of congressional, state legislative, and local government election districts to favor one person, interest, or political party over another has been an unfair and wasteful part of the redistricting process in this state as far back as electoral history will take us. Too often, however, observers tend to see only the bizarrely shaped districts as gerrymanders. In fact, some of the most unfairly drawn districts in Texas history and worldwide were not irregular in appearance. A gerrymandered district may be aesthetically attractive but, like the perfectly rectangular 5th congressional district in Dallas (that by 1960 was almost 4.4 times the population of the neighboring 4th congressional district), is designed to advantage or disadvantage political groups. A district's appearance may hide its unfair purpose or effect.

The United States alone in the world today has a firm "one person, one vote" requirement that is strictly enforced by the courts. Within the constraints of such a policy, the magnitude of the electoral harm from even the most grotesquely shaped gerrymander is limited. Moreover, gerrymanders are not guaranteed to succeed. The first election district so wrought—in 1812 by the Massachusetts Legislature and Governor Elbridge Gerry—testifies to this inconclusiveness. If this gerrymander was intended to allow Governor Gerry's Democratic-Republican Party to win the district, it was a failure; the Democratic-Republican candidate lost. If, however, its purpose was to pack Federalist voters in the district so that Gerry's party could win elsewhere, it was a success. The Democratic-Republican Party won a majority of seats in the Massachusetts Senate. The targeted Federalist incumbent congressman was reelected.

Likewise, when Patrick Henry successfully led an attempt in the Virginia Legislature to draw a congressional district in which James Madison was not expected to win, Madison won anyway. The names in Texas history that were the targets of gerrymanders are not so illustrious, but this state's history is full of surprises and occasions when a Democratic or Republican majority in the legislature has drawn election districts expecting a certain electoral outcome only to see its plans go awry.

It is in the context of reducing the effect of gerrymanders that I reemphasize the importance of the "one person, one vote" principle. No redistricting plan can subvert the public will forever if this principle, along with the Voting Rights Act, is vigorously enforced. Redistricting in equally populated electoral districts is a risky, zero-sum exercise. A redistricting plan drawn to create "safe" legislative seats for one party or group almost always also creates similar districts for the other party. A plan that attempts to maximize a party's or group's power by creating a large number of districts with a small majority of that party's or group's voters in a maximum number of districts creates a risk that a change in public mood may cause the party to lose in most or all of these districts. Time changes results—although the change may occur slowly.

Some gerrymanders may even be seen as helpful for achieving legally approved public policy goals. Among the most lasting gerrymanders in Texas history are ones that have their origin in attempts by the state, local governments, or the courts to comply with federal law by drawing districts that afford African American and Hispanic residents an equal opportunity to elect a person of their choice. Such districts have proven to be effective, allowing a state without a single African American or Hispanic in its state legislature or congressional delegation at the beginning of the twentieth century to have over seventy serving by the end of the century. The impact on politics and policymaking from this change has been enormous but may be less necessary now than in the past.

On the other hand, gerrymanders may be used to suppress the vote of minorities that have suffered past discrimination and, as a result, have unequal access to the political process.

Much of the litigation over the past seventy years has been directed at righting this wrong. These gerrymanders for partisan advantage often come disguised as districts designed to benefit minorities.

EFFORTS TO MARGINALIZE THE DEMOCRATIC PARTY

One of the most lasting and disturbing vestiges of recent gerrymandering is the possible long-term marginalization of the Democratic Party by sucking non-Hispanic white voters and candidates out of the party. In the words of Republican political activist Grover Norquist, "[No] Texan need grow up thinking that being a Democrat is acceptable behavior."

As described earlier, the Republican strategy in 2003 was to target all ten of the non-Hispanic white Democratic incumbents to make the face of the Democratic delegation solely people of color. The overall change in the demographics of the party is a welcome contrast to the years of non-Hispanic white dominance and voter repression. For some Democrats, however, it is alarming if it adversely affects hope for a Democratic comeback in Texas.

> In 2001, there was a 78-member Democratic majority in the Texas House of Representatives. After the 2002 election, this figure dropped to a 62-member minority. In 2011, the number of Democrats in the House dropped to forty-nine (with 101 Republicans). Only eight of those Democratic representatives were non-Hispanic whites.

> In 2003, there were seventeen Democrats and fifteen Republicans in Congress from Texas. Ten non-Hispanic white Democrats were targeted for defeat by Republicans in the 2003 redistricting. Eight of the ten were no longer in Congress as Democrats by the end of the decade, but one non-Hispanic white, Beto O'Rourke, won election in a district that had previously elected a Hispanic Democrat. In 2018, two of the new Democrats were African American or Hispanic.

In 2003, there were twelve Democrats in the Texas Senate. In 2019, there were still twelve, but only four of these Democratic senators were non-Hispanic white.

According to *The Texas Tribune*, 80 percent of the Democrats in the 86th Legislature (House and senate) are persons of color.

For Republicans, this trend is welcome. From the perspective of political consultant Karl Rove, this phenomenon was not due to any Republican strategy but instead showed a shift of the non-Hispanic white electorate to the Republican Party ideology and the foreseeable result under Section 5 of the Voting Rights Act of intentionally drawing districts to give African American and Hispanic voters the ability to elect persons of their choice.

Whatever the cause of this change, it is possible that by the near future there will be no non-Hispanic white Democrat in Congress from Texas and few in the state legislature. The election results in 2018, however, showed the possibility of a reversal of this trend. In 2019, there were sixty-seven Democrats in the House of Representatives, with nine of the seventeen newly elected Democrats being non-Hispanic white. Two of the three new Democratic senators elected in 2020 were non-Hispanic white. In 2019, the Texas congressional delegation consisted of twenty-three Republicans and thirteen Democrats. Although only three of these Democrats were non-Hispanic whites, one of the newly elected Democrats was non-Hispanic white and replaced a Republican. Two non-Hispanic white Democrats, Gene Green and Beto O'Rourke, voluntarily did not seek reelection and were replaced by Hispanic Democrats. African American Democrat Colin Allred unseated a Republican incumbent.

The longer-term demographic trends suggest that a party consisting almost entirely of non-Hispanic whites cannot maintain majority status. Diversity among party membership should be a goal for both major parties. Texas experienced the wrongs of one-party rule for over 100 years; it does not need to do so again. A competitive multi-party election system is in the public interest.

REDISTRICTING COMMISSIONS

While I believe Texas history demonstrates that redistricting by the legislature is dominated by political and individual self-interest, merely claiming that self-interest is avoided by having a redistricting commission is simplistic. The commission must be truly independent of political self-interest. Most so-called "independent" commissions are not truly independent. It is foolish to think that simply allowing independent commissions rather than the legislature to redistrict is a means of both eliminating gerrymandering and reducing partisan gridlock. The actual record of such commissions achieving these goals is mixed at best.

The precise number of independent redistricting commissions now in use nationwide is a product of a surveyor's definition of what constitutes an independent commission. For example, Texas has an "independent" commission in some counts because it has the Texas Legislative Redistricting Board, which consists of four statewide elected officials and the Speaker of the House of Representatives. This commission was originally considered a reform, but it has become a political weapon.

Moreover, some commissions, such as the LRB, lack jurisdiction over congressional redistricting. Others simply prepare a plan that then goes to the state legislature for adoption or rejection. There are twelve states with "independent" commissions entrusted with actual line-drawing authority. Only six of these have responsibility for drawing both state legislative and congressional districts.

The largest number of these "independent" commissions are the ten so-called bipartisan commissions that have an equal number of Republicans and Democrats, along with an unaffiliated component that acts as a tiebreaker if needed. This count was made in 2014 and did not include the "citizen redistricting commissions" in California and Arizona. The biggest difficulty in the past for bipartisan commissions is that they have themselves been products of legislation passed by a partisan legislature. With their members generally appointed by politicians, these commissions have sometimes produced partisan fairness but at the cost of institutionalizing partisanship as the primary consideration in redistricting by adopting plans that protect incumbents of both parties. Of these ten bipartisan commissions, six saw their plans declared invalid in 2011–2013. The problem was that the commissions had violated the neutral criteria set by state law. These commissions were probably trying to reach an agreeable bipartisan plan that protected the incumbents of both parties.

In an effort to combat this partisanship, some states have used judges, in office or retired, in determining the composition of the commission. Opponents of this alternative in Texas point out that this state's judges are also elected in partisan elections. In California, the commission was created through a petition and voter referendum without the participation of the state legislature. California's "Citizen Commission," which was created by referendum in 2008, consists of "citizens" generally selected at random from pools of qualified applicants. Austin, Texas, followed the California model and through a petition and referendum adopted a citizen commission in 2014. The State of Texas, however, lacks the vehicle of a public petition and referendum, so any change must come through legislation approved by the legislature.

Many members of the Texas Legislature object to an independent commission altogether because they feel that no commission can possibly represent the diversity of interests and perspectives present in a legislative body. For several sessions, State Senator Jeff Wentworth tried unsuccessfully to pass legislation that would create an independent commission in Texas. Now, Senator Wentworth is gone from the legislature. Recent efforts at creation of a commission have failed.

Texas cannot be free of political gerrymandering while the members of the Texas Legislature draw their own districts. Redistricting will remain a grab for power highlighted by self-interest and hollow justifications of never-ending "payback" and revenge for earlier wrongs. I, therefore, think that a redistricting commission is appropriate, but it must be truly independent in its authority both to enact a redistricting plan without legislative approval and to act without political influence. Many examples exist worldwide.

A NEED FOR NEUTRAL REDISTRICTING CRITERIA

Many jurisdictions have legally required neutral criteria for redistricting, such as requirements that electoral districts must be contiguous, compact, and equal in population; respect political subdivision boundaries; consider natural features (e.g., mountains, bodies of water, etc.); and keep communities of interest intact. These criteria represent the public-interest component of redistricting.

The Texas Constitution establishes only a few such criteria. Article III, Section 25, provides: "The State shall be divided into Senatorial Districts of contiguous territory, and each district shall be entitled to elect one Senator." Section 26 of Article III provides: "The members of the House of Representatives shall be apportioned among the several counties, according to the number of population in each . . . " with a few exceptions. There are no criteria for congressional districts.

This paucity of neutral criteria leaves Texas with gerrymandered congressional and senate districts that meander across the state, divide counties haphazardly, and are dictated primarily by political self-interest. No neutral criteria govern the drawing of state House of Representative districts.

I suggest the following provisions be added to the Texas Constitution:

Section ___: Senate electoral districts shall be compact, contiguous, and equal in population. Each district to the extent possible shall be composed (1) of whole counties except as necessary to equalize population or (2) to include part of a city that is divided by county lines. In a county entitled by its population to two or more Senate districts, only one district may cross county lines. The requirements of this section shall continue to apply to the extent that they are not in conflict with federal law or the US Constitution.

Section___: Congressional electoral districts shall be compact, contiguous, and equal in population. Each district to the extent possible shall be composed of whole counties except (1) as necessary to equalize population or (2) to include part of a city that is divided by county lines. In a county entitled by its population to two or more congressional districts, only one district may cross county lines. The requirements of this section shall continue to apply to the extent that they are not in conflict with federal law or the US Constitution.

To reduce the influence of political self-interest on the drawing of electoral districts, I suggest adding the following constitutional provision:

Section ___: The boundaries of congressional, State Senate, or State House electoral districts may not be drawn for the purpose of advantaging or disadvantaging any person or group except as required by federal law or the United States Constitution. No public money shall be spent to provide any data intended to show the likely election outcome in any district.

CONCLUSION

Courts have been an invaluable tool for bringing needed changes in the Texas election system. Litigation, however, is a costly, protracted, and sometimes ham-fisted endeavor. It should be a last resort, not an expected part of the redistricting process. Self-interest must be eliminated from how electoral districts are drawn, not just remedied afterward. Texas can do better.

Politics is never static. Whether, or when, Democrats once again gain control of the Texas Legislature and statewide elected offices, or whether Republicans or some third party will rule these elections forever, is uncertain. The effects of the redistricting controlled by Republicans in 2021 will be felt throughout the decade and beyond, but the precise nature of those effects will remain unknown even after the final plans are adopted. In this circumstance, the greatest safeguard of the supremacy of the public remains rigorous enforcement of the principle of one person, one vote.

POSTSCRIPT

THIS BOOK CONSISTS LARGELY of material first written in fall 2010 for the Constitutional Law II: Redistricting Texas class at the University of Texas School of Law, which I taught.

In that course, I focused specifically on redistricting and on the Texas experience. This book is an outgrowth of that project. My objective remained to provide my students with a full understanding of the law applicable to redistricting. Necessarily, this meant covering the important US Supreme Court decisions. In this book, however, I undertook to show the law and those Supreme Court cases in the context of the reality of their effect on events in Texas rather than merely from the text of the Supreme Court opinions themselves. I hope the examination of the cases, personalities, and politics that determined the real outcomes and changes in Texas will provide the reader a meaningful learning experience.

A book like this is uniquely focused. Admittedly, however, it is an experiment. Fortunately, Bob Heath and I were involved in many of the most significant state and local redistricting cases in Texas of the past four decades. This first-hand experience has made the task somewhat easier and has allowed us in a few circumstances to go beyond the official events and to write about happenings behind the scenes.

A few notes for the reader: (1) The original material for the law school class included edited copies of many of the major cases. Those have been deleted. (2) A list of authorities is included at the end of the book. I chose not to cram the book with unnecessary citations or political theories. (3)

A chapter on the redistricting of local governments in Texas (e.g., counties, cities, school districts) was deleted from this book. A worthwhile discussion of this subject deserves much more than a chapter.

STEVE BICKERSTAFF

APPENDIX

UNITED STATES CONSTITUTION, ARTICLE I

Section 2. [T]he electors in each state shall have the qualifications requisite for electors of the most numerous branch of the State Legislature . . . . Representatives . . . shall be apportioned among the several states . . . according to their respective numbers . . . . The actual Enumeration . . . shall be made within . . . every . . . term of ten years, in such manner as they [the Congress of the United States] shall by law direct.

Section 4. The times, places and Manner of holding elections for Senators and Representatives, shall be prescribed in each state by the Legislature thereof; but the Congress may at any time by law make or alter such regulations, except as to the places of choosing senators.

FOURTEENTH AMENDMENT OF THE UNITED STATES CONSTITUTION (RATIFIED IN 1868)

Section 1. All persons born or naturalized in the United States, and subject to the jurisdiction thereof, are citizens of the United States and the State wherein they reside. No State shall make or enforce any law which shall abridge the privileges or immunities of citizens of the United States; nor shall any State deprive any person of life, liberty, or property, without due process of law; nor deny to any person within its jurisdiction the equal protection of the laws.

Section 2. Representatives shall be apportioned among the several States according to their respective numbers.

FIFTEENTH AMENDMENT OF THE UNITED STATES CONSTITUTION (RATIFIED IN 1870)

Section 1. The right of citizens of the United States to vote shall not be denied or abridged by the United States or by any state on account of race, color, or previous condition of servitude.

TEXAS CONSTITUTION OF 1866, ARTICLE III

Section 1. Every free male person who shall have attained the age of twenty-one years, and who shall be a citizen of the United States, and shall have resided in this State one year next preceding an election, and the last six months within the district, county, city or town in which he offers to vote, (Indians not taxed, Africans and descendants of Africans excepted,) shall be deemed a qualified elector; and should such qualified elector happen to be in any other county situated in the district in which he resides at the time of an election, he shall be permitted to vote for any district officer; provided, that the qualified electors shall be permitted to vote anywhere in the State for State officers; and provided further, that no soldier, seaman or marine, in the army or navy of the United States, shall be entitled to vote at any election created by this Constitution.

Section 2. Electors in all cases shall be privileged from arrest during their attendance at elections, and in going to and returning from the same, except in cases of treason, felony or breach of the peace.

Section 3. The Legislative powers of this State shall be vested in two distinct branches, the one to be styled the Senate, and the other the House of Representatives, and both together the "Legislature of the State of Texas." The style of all laws shall be, "Be it enacted by the Legislature of the State of Texas."

Section 4. The members of the House of Representatives shall be chosen by the qualified electors, and their term of office shall be two years from the day of the general election, and the sessions of the Legislature shall be biennial at such times as shall be prescribed by law.

Section 5. No person shall be a representative unless he be a white citizen of the United States, and shall be a qualified elector at the time of his election, and a resident of the State for five years, next preceding his election, and the last year thereof a citizen of the county, city, town or district for which he shall be chosen.

TEXAS CONSTITUTION OF 1876, ARTICLE III

Section 25. The State shall be divided into senatorial districts of contiguous territory according to the number of qualified electors, as nearly as may be, and each district shall be entitled to elect one senator, and no single county shall be entitled to more than one senator. [This is the section as adopted in 1876; it was amended to remove the reference to "qualified electors" and the limit of one senate district per county.]

Section 26. The members of the House of Representatives shall be apportioned among the several counties, according to the number of population in each, as nearly as may be, on a ratio obtained by dividing the population of the State, as ascertained by the most recent United States census, by the number of members of which the house is composed; provided, that, whenever a single county has sufficient population to be entitled to a representative, such county shall be formed into a separate representative district, and when two or more counties are required to make up the ratio of representation such counties shall be contiguous to each other; and when any one county has more than sufficient population to be entitled to one or more representatives, such representative or representatives shall be apportioned to such county, and for any surplus of population it may be joined in a representative district with any other contiguous county or counties.

Section 26a [as adopted in 1936]. Provided however, that no county shall be entitled to or have under any apportionment more than seven (7) Representatives. [This amendment was declared violative of the United States Constitution in 1965 and subsequently repealed.]

Section 28 [as amended in 1949]. The Legislature shall, at its first regular session after the publication of each United States decennial census, apportion the state into senatorial and representative districts, agreeable to the provisions of Sections 25 and 26 of this Article. In the event the Legislature shall at any such first regular session following the publication of a United States decennial census, fail to make such apportionment, same shall be done by the Legislative Redistricting Board of Texas, which is hereby created, and shall be composed of five (5) members, as follows: The Lieutenant Governor, the Speaker of the House of Representatives, the Attorney General, the Comptroller of Public Accounts and the Commissioner of the General Land Office, a majority of whom shall constitute a quorum. Said Board shall assemble in the City of Austin within ninety (90) days after the final adjournment of such regular session. The Board shall, within sixty (60) days after assembling, apportion the state into senatorial and representative districts, or into senatorial or representative districts, as the failure of action of such Legislature may make necessary. Such apportionment shall be in writing and signed by three or more of the members of the Board duly acknowledged as the act and deed of such Board, and, when so executed and filed with the Secretary of State, shall have force and effect of law. Such apportionment shall become effective at the next succeeding statewide general election. The Supreme Court of Texas shall have jurisdiction to compel such Board to perform its duties in accordance with the provisions of this section by writ of mandamus or other extraordinary writs conformable to the usages of law. The Legislature shall provide necessary funds for clerical and technical aid and for other expenses incidental to the work of the Board, and the Lieutenant Governor and the Speaker of the House of Representatives shall be entitled to receive per diem and travel expense during the Board's session in the same manner and amount as they would receive while attending a special session of the Legislature.

Article VI, Suffrage [as adopted]

Section 1. The following classes of persons shall not be allowed to vote in this State, to wit: First—Persons under twenty-one years of age.

Second—Idiots and lunatics.

Third—All paupers supported by any county.

Fourth—All persons convicted of any felony, subject to such exceptions as the Legislature may make.

Fifth—All soldiers, marines and seamen, employed in the service of the army or navy of the United States.

Section 2. Every male person subject to none of the foregoing disqualifications, who shall have attained the age of
twenty-one years, and who shall be a citizen of the United
States, and who shall have resided in this State one year
next preceding an election, and the last six months within the district or county in which he offers to vote, shall
be deemed a qualified elector; and every male person of
foreign birth, subject to none of the foregoing disqualifications, who, at any time before an election, shall have
declared his intention to become a citizen of the United
States, in accordance with the federal naturalization laws,
and shall have resided in this State one year next preceding such election, and the last six months in the county in
which he offers to vote, shall also be deemed a qualified
elector; and all electors shall vote in the election precinct
of their residence; provided, that electors living in any
unorganized county, may vote at any election precinct in
the county to which such county is attached, for judicial
purposes.

Section 3. All qualified electors of the State, as herein
described, who shall have resided for six months immediately preceding an election within the limits of any city
or corporate town, shall have the right to vote for mayor
and all other elective officers; but in all elections to determine expenditure of money or assumption of debt, only
those shall be qualified to vote who pay taxes on property in said city or incorporated town; provided, that no
poll tax for the payment of debts thus incurred, shall be
levied upon the persons debarred from voting in relation
thereto.

[Article VI of the Texas Constitution of 1876 has largely
been nullified or repealed.]

VOTING RIGHTS ACT OF 1965 [AS AMENDED]

Section 2. (52 U.S.C. Sec. 10301): No voting qualification . . . or . . . practice . . . shall be imposed . . . by any State or political subdivision in a manner which results in a denial or abridgement of the right of any citizen . . . to vote on account of race or color, or in contravention of the guarantees (for language minorities) as provided in subsection (b).

A violation of subsection (a) is established if, based on the totality of the circumstances, it is shown that the political processes leading to nomination or election in the State or political subdivision are not equally open to participation by members of a class of citizens protected by subsection (a) in that its members have less opportunity than other members of the electorate to participate in the political process and to elect representatives of their choice. The extent to which members of a protected class have been elected to office in the State or political subdivision is one circumstance which may be considered: Provided, that nothing in this section establishes a right to have members of a protected class elected in numbers equal to their proportion in the population.

Section 4. (52 U.S.C. Sec. 10303): To ensure that the right of citizens of the United States to vote is not denied or abridged on account of race or color, no citizen shall be denied the right to vote in any Federal, State or local election because of his failure to comply with any test or device in any State with respect to which the determinations have been made (under this section) . . . unless the United States District Court for the District of Columbia issues a declaratory judgment under this section . . .

(e) (These subsections generally define the "test or device" prohibited in subsection (a), provide for the factual determinations that must be made to subject a State or political subdivision [i.e., a "covered jurisdiction"] to this section and Section 5 of the act, and set out the conditions that must be met to bail out of such coverage)

(f) (1) . . . .

No voting qualification . . . or . . . practice . . . shall be imposed or applied by any State or political subdivision to deny or abridge the right of any citizen of the United States to vote because he is a member of a language minority.

In addition to the meaning given the term (elsewhere) . . . the term "test or device" shall also mean any practice or requirement by which any State or political subdivision provided (election materials) . . . only in the English language, where the Director of the Census determines that more than five per centum of the citizens of voting age . . . are members of a single language minority . . .

Whenever any State or political subdivision subject to [this section] provides any [election materials] . . . it shall provide them in the language of the applicable language minority group as well as in the English language, where the Director of the Census determines that more than five per centum of the citizens of voting age . . . are members of a single language minority . . .

[The addition of Subsection 4 (f) in 1975 made Texas subject to Section 5 of the Act]

Section 5. (52 U.S.C. Sec. 10304) [as amended in 2006]: Whenever a State or political subdivision [covered by the prohibitions in Section 4(a)] shall enact or seek to administer any voting qualification . . . or . . . practice with respect to voting different from that in force or effect [when this section became applicable to the state or political subdivision] . . . such State or political subdivision may institute an action in the United States District Court for the District of Columbia for a declaratory judgment that such qualification . . . or . . . practice . . . neither has the purpose nor will have the effect of denying or abridging the right to vote on account of race or color, or (for a language minority) . . . and unless and until the court enters such judgment no person shall be denied the right to vote for failure to comply with such qualification . . . or . . . practice . . . : Provided, that such qualification . . . or . . . practice . . . may be enforced . . . if . . . submitted . . . to the Attorney General and the Attorney General has not interposed an objection within sixty days after such submission or . . . the Attorney General has affirmatively indicated that such objection will not be made . . . . Any action under this section shall be heard and determined by a court of three judges . . .

Any voting qualification . . . or . . . practice . . . that has the purpose of or will have the effect of diminishing the ability of any citizens of the United States on account of race or color, or (for a language minority), to elect their preferred candidates of choice denies or abridges the right to vote within the meaning of subsection (b) of this section.

The term "purpose" in subsections (a) and (b) of this section shall include any discriminatory purpose.

The purpose of subsection (b) is to protect the ability of such citizens to elect their preferred candidates of choice.

[In 2014, the US Supreme Court ruled in *Shelby County v. Holder* that the formula in Section 4 of the act was no longer valid. This ruling effectively nullified the preclearance requirement of Section 5.]

BIBLIOGRAPHY

Banks, Jimmy. *Gavels, Grit, and Glory; The Billy Clayton Story.* Fort Worth, TX: Eakin Press, 1981.

Bickerstaff, Steve. "Effects of the Voting Rights Act on Reapportionment and Hispanic Voting Strength in Texas." *University of Texas Hispanic Journal of Law and Policy* 6(1), Summer 2001: 99–122.

———. *Lines in the Sand: Congressional Redistricting in Texas and the Downfall of Tom Delay.* Austin: University of Texas Press, 2007.

———. "Reapportionment by State Legislatures: A Guide for the 1980s." SMU Law Review 34, no. 2 (1980): 607–686.

———. "Voting Rights Challenges to School Boards in Texas" Baylor Law Review 49 (Fall 1997): 1017–56.

Braden, George D., ed. *The Constitution of Texas: An Annotated and Comparative Analysis.* Austin: Texas Advisory Commission on Intergovernmental Relations, 1977.

Calvert, Robert W. *Here Comes the Judge: From State Home to State House.* Waco, TX: Texian Press, 1977.

Chumlea, W. S. *The Politics of Legislative Apportionment in Texas, 1921–1957.* Austin: University of Texas Press, 1959.

Fehrenbach, T. R. *Lone Star: A History of Texas and the Texans.* New York: Wings Books, 1968.

Keith, Gary A., ed. *Rotten Boroughs, Political Thickets, and Legislative Donnybrooks: Redistricting in Texas.* Austin: University of Texas Press, 2013.

Kemerer, Frank R. *William Wayne Justice: A Judicial Biography.* Austin: University of Texas Press, 1991.

Levinson, Sanford. "One Person, One Vote: A Mantra in Need of Meaning." *North Carolina Law Review* 80 (2002): 1269–97.

Richards, David. *Once Upon a Time in Texas: A Liberal in the Lone Star State*. Austin: University of Texas Press, 2002.

Texas State Historical Association. *Handbook of African American Texas*, 2018.

———. *Handbook of Tejano History*, 2016.

———. *Texas Almanac 2018–2019*, 2018.

Young, John Hardin, ed. *International Election Principles: Democracy & the Rule of Law*. American Bar Association, 2009.

WEBSITES

Ballotpedia (www.ballotpedia.org)

Texas Demographic Center (www.demographics.texas.gov)

Texas Legislative Council (www.tlc.texas.gov)

Texas Legislative Reference Library (www.lrl.texas.gov)

Texas Legislature Online (www.capitol.texas.gov)

Texas Secretary of State (www.sos.state.tx.us)

Texas State Library and Archives Commission (www.tsl.texas.gov/contact)

Texas Tribune (www.texastribune.org)

US Bureau of Census (www.census.gov)

LEGAL AUTHORITIES

General

Journals for the Constitutional Conventions of 1836, 1845, 1861, 1869, 1875

Texas Constitution of 1836, Article I, Sections 5 and 7

Texas Constitution of 1845, Article III, Sections 10, 13, and 29

Texas Constitution of 1866, Article III, Sections 1–5, 28 and 40

Texas Constitution of 1876, Article III, Sections 2, 25, 26, 26a, and 28; Article VI

Statewide Redistricting Cases and Authority
1836–1960

Smith v. Patterson, 242 S.W. 749 (Tex. 1922)

Nixon v. Herndon, 273 U.S. 536 (1927)

Nixon v. Condon, 286 U.S. 79 (1932)

Grovey v. Townsend, 295 U.S. 45 (1935)

Smith v. Allwright, 321 U.S. 649 (1944)

Colegrove v. Green, 328 U.S. 549 (1946)

Op. Tex. Att'y Gen. No. V-53 (1952)

Terry v. Adams, 345 U.S. 461 (1953)

Gomillion v. Lightfoot, 364 U.S. 339 (1960)

1961–1970

Baker v. Carr, 369 U.S. 186 (1962)

Gray v. Sanders, 372. U.S. 368 (1963)

Bush v. Martin (Bush I), 224 F.Supp.499 (S.D. Tex. 1963), aff'd per curium, 376 U.S. 222 (1964)

Miller v. James, 366 S.W. 118 (Tex. Civ. App.—Austin 1963, no writ)

Lucas v. Forty-Fourth General Assembly of Colorado, 377 U.S. 733 (1964)

Reynolds v. Sims, 377 U.S. 533 (1964)

Wesberry v. Sanders, 376 U.S. 1 (1964)

Hainsworth v. Martin, 386 S.W.2d (Tex. Civ. App.–Austin, writ ref'd n.r.e.), vacated as moot, 382 U.S. 109 (1965)

Kilgarlin v. Martin, No. 63-H-390 (S.D. Tex. Jan. 11, 1965)

Burns v. Richardson, 384 U.S. 73 (1966)

Bush v. Martin (Bush II), 251 F.Supp. 484 (S.D. Tex. 1966)

Kilgarlin v. Martin, 252 F.Supp. 404 (S.D. Tex. 1966)

South Carolina v. Katzenbach, 383 U.S. 701 (1966)

Kilgarlin v. Hill, 386 U.S. 120 (1967)

Allen v. State Board of Education, 393 U.S. 544 (1969)

Kirkpatrick v. Preisler, 394 U.S. 526 (1969)

1971–1980

Connor v. Johnson, 402 U.S. 690 (1971)

Mauzy v. Legislative Redistricting Board, 471 S.W. 570 (Tex. 1971)

Perkins v. Mathews, 400 U.S. 379 (1971)

Smith v. Craddick, 471 S.W.2d 375 (Tex. 1971)

Graves v. Barnes (Graves I), 343 F.Supp. 704 (W.D. Tex. 1972), aff'd sub nom. Archer v. Smith, 409 U.S. 808 (1972), modified sub nom. White v. Regester, 412 U.S. 755 (1973)

Gaffney v. Cummings, 412 U.S. 735 (1973)

Mahon v. Howell, 410 U.S. 315 (1973)

White v. Regester, 412 U.S. 755 (1973)

White v. Weiser, 412 U.S. 783 (1973)

Zimmer v. McKeithen, 485 F.2d 1297 (5th Cir. 1973)

Graves v. Barnes (Graves II), 378 F.Supp. 640 (W.D. Tex. 1974), remanded for determination of mootness sub nom. White v. Regester, 422 U.S. 935 (1975)

City of Richmond v. United States, 422 U.S. 358 (1975)

White v. Regester, 422 U.S. 935 (1975)

Graves v. Barnes (Graves III), 408 F.Supp. 1050 (W.D. Tex. 1976)

United Jewish Organizations of Williamsburg v. Carey, 430 U.S. 144 (1977)

Beer v. United States, 425 U.S. 130 (1978)

Graves v. Barnes (Graves IV), 446 F.Supp. 560 (W.D. Tex.), aff'd sub nom. Briscoe v. Escalante, 435 U.S. 901 (1978)

City of Mobile v. Bolden, 446 U.S. 55 (1980)

City of Rome v. United States, 446 U.S. 156 (1980)

1981–1990

Clements v. Valles, 620 S.W.2d 112 (Tex. 1981)

McDaniel v. Sanchez, 452 U.S. 130 (1981)

Rogers v. Lodge, 458 U.S. 613 (1982)

Seamon v. Upham, 536 F.Supp. 1030 (E.D. Tex. 1982)

Terrazas v. Clements, 513 F.Supp. 514 (1982)

Upham v. Seamon, 456 U.S. 37 (1982)

Upham v. Seamon, 639 S.W.2d 301 (Tex. 1982)

Karcher v. Daggett, 462 U.S. 725 (1983)

Terrazas v. Clements, 581 F.Supp. 1329 (N.D. Tex. 1984)

Davis v. Bandemer, 478 U.S. 109 (1986)

Thornburg v. Gingles, 478 U.S. 30 (1986)

City of Pleasant Grove v. United States, 479 U.S. 462 (1987)

Board of Estimate of New York v. Morris, 489 U.S. 688 (1989)

1991–2000

Chisom v. Roemer, 501 U.S. 380 (1991)

Clark v. Roemer, 500 U.S. 646 (1991)

Garza v. County of Los Angeles, 98 F.2d 763 (9th Cir. 1991)

Terrazas v. Ramirez, 829 S.W.2d 712 (Tex. 1991)

Presley v. Etowah County Comm., 502 U.S. 491 (1992)

State of Texas v. U.S., 785 F.Supp. 201 (DDC 1992)

State of Texas v. U.S., 802 F.Supp. 481 (DDC 1992)

Terrazas v. Slagle, 789 F.Supp. 828 (W.D. Tex. 1992)

Growe v. Emison, 507 U.S. 25 (1993)

LULAC v. Clements, 999 F.2d 831 (5th Cir. 1993)

Shaw v. Reno, 509 U.S. 630 (1993)

Voinovich v. Quilter, 507 U.S. 146 (1993)

Holder v. Hall, 512 U.S. 874 (1994)

Johnson v. DeGrandy, 512 U.S. 997 (1994)

Vera v. Richards, 861 F.Supp. 1304 (S.D. Tex. 1994)

DeWitt v. Wilson, 515 U.S. 1170 (1995)

DeWitt v. Wilson, 856 F.Supp. 1409 (E.D. Cal. 1995)

Miller v. Johnson, 515 U.S. 900 (1995)

Bush v. Vera, 517 U.S. 952 (1996)

Vera v. Bush, 933 F.Supp. 1341 (S.D. Tex. 1996)

Abrams v. Johnson, 521 U.S. 74 (1997)

Armbrister v. Morales, 943 S.W.2d 202 (Tex. App.— Austin, 1997, no writ) (enactment by legislature of court-ordered plan is not new apportionment requiring election of senators who are in the middle of staggered terms)

City of Boerne v. United States, 521 U.S. 507 (1997)

Lawyer v. Dept. of Justice, 521 U.S. 567 (1997)

Terrazas v. Slagle, 821 F.Supp. 1162 (W.D. Tex. 1997)

Vera v. Bush, 980 F.Supp. 251 (S.D. Tex. 1997)

Department of Commerce v. United States House of Representatives, 525 U.S. 316 (1999)

Hunt v. Cromartie, 526 U.S. 541 (1999)

Lopez v. Monterey County, 525 U.S. 266 (1999)

Reno v. Bossier Parish School Board, 528 U.S. 320 (2000)

2001–2010

Easley v. Cromartie, 532 U.S. 234 (2001)

Perry v. Del Rio, 66 S.W.3d 239 (Tex. 2001)

Perry v. Del Rio, 67 S.W.3d 85 (Tex. 2001)

Branch v. Smith, 538 U.S. 254 (2003)

Georgia v. Ashcroft, 539 U.S. 526 (2003)

Cox v. Larios, 542 U.S. 947 (2004)

Larios v. Cox, 300 F.Supp.2d 1320 (N.D. Georgia 2004)

Larios v. Cox, 314 F.Supp.2d 1357 (N.D. Georgia 2004)

Session v. Perry, 298 F.Supp.2d 451 (E.D. Tex. 2004)

Vieth v. Jubelirer, 541 U.S. 267 (2004)

Henderson v. Perry, 399 F.Supp. 756 (E.D. Tex. 2005)

League of United Latin American Citizens v. Perry, 548 U.S. 399 (2006)

League of United Latin American Citizens v. Perry, 457 F.Supp.2d 716 (E.D. Tex. 2006)

Northwest Austin Municipal Utility District v. Holder, 557 U.S. 193 (2009)

2011–2019

Perry v. Perez, 835 F.Supp.2d 209 (2011)

Perez v. Perry, 565 U.S. 388 (2012)

Texas v. United States, 887 F.Supp.2d 133 (2012)

Shelby County v. Holder, 570 U.S. 529 (2013)

Davis v. Perry, Davis v. Abbott, 781 F.3d 207 (5th Cir. 2015)

Evenwel v. Abbott, 578 U.S. ___, 136 S.Ct. 1120 (2016)

Perez v. Abbott, 267 F.Supp.3d 750 and 274 F.Supp.3d 624 (2017)

Abbott v. Perez, 585 U.S. ___, 138 S.Ct. 2305 (2018)

Perez v. Abbott, 390 F.Supp.3d 803 (2019)

Rucho v. Common Cause, ___U.S.___, 139 S.Ct. 2484 (2019)

United States Department of Commerce v. New York, ___U.S.___, 139 S.Ct. 2551 (2019)

Local Government Redistricting Cases

Dubose v. Woods, 162 S.W. 3 (Tex. Civ. App.–San Antonio 1913, no writ)

Williams v. Woods, 162 S.W. 1031 (Tex. Civ. App.–San Antonio 1914, no writ)

Avery v. Midland County, 406 S.W.2d 422 (Tex. 1966)

Avery v. Midland County, 390 U.S. 474 (1968)

Hereford I.S.D. v. Bell, 454 F.Supp. 143 (N.D. Tex. 1975)

Wilson v. Vahue, 403 F.Supp. 58 (N.D. Tex. 1975)

Wise v. Lipscomb, 399 F.Supp. 782 (N.D. Texas 1975)

Greater Houston Civic Council v. Mann, 440 F.Supp. 696 (S.D. Tex. 1977)

Gumfory v. Hansford County Commissioner's. Ct., 561 S.W.2d 28 (Tex. Civ. App.—Amarillo 1977, writ ref'd n.r.e.)

Wise v. Lipscomb, 437 U.S. 535 (1978)

Calderon v. McGee, 589 F.2d 909 (5th Cir. 1979)

Ramos v. Koebig, 638 F.2d 838 (5th Cir. 1981)

City of Port Arthur v. United States, 517 F.Supp. 987 (DDC 1981)

City of Port Arthur v. United States, 459 U.S. 159 (1981)

Campos v. City of Baytown, 840 F.2d 1240 (5th Cir. 1988)

Overton v. City of Austin, 871 F.2d 529 (5th Cir. 1989)

Williams v. City of Dallas, 73 F.Supp. 1317 (N.D. Tex. 1990)

Salas v. Southwest Texas Junior College, 964 F.2d 1542 (5th Cir. 1992)

Morris v. City of Houston, 894 F.Supp. 1062 (S.D. Tex. 1995)

Concerned Citizens for Equality v. McDonald, 63 F.3d 413 (5th Cir. 1995)

LULAC v. Northeast I.S.D., 903 F.Supp. 1071 (W.D. Tex. 1995)

Campos v. City of Houston, 113 F.3d 544 (5th Cir. 1997)

Perez v. Pasadena I.S.D., 956 F.Supp. 1196 (S.D. Tex. 1997)

Chen v. City of Houston, 9 F.Supp. 2d 745 (E.D. Tex. 1998)

Valdespino v. Alamo Heights I.S.D., 168 F.3d 848 (5th Cir. 1999)

Chen v. City of Houston, 206 F.3d 502 (5th Cir. 2000)

INDEX

Abbott, Gregory, 13, 141–42, 144, 160, 174, 176
Abbott v. Perez (2018), 165, 171
Abner, David, 58
African Americans: cohesiveness of, 202–3; in Congress, 100–101, 128; and Democratic strategy for 2021, 194–97; at 1869 Constitutional Convention, 55–56; at 1876 Constitutional Convention, 58; emergence as political force in Republican Party, 59–60; and failure of 1991 Democratic redistricting strategy, 116–18; increased congressional representation for, in 1990s, 121; and liberal Democratic and minority litigation strategy, 118–20; and litigation over 1981 reapportionment of congressional districts, 111; remedying past discrimination against, 204–5; rights of post-Civil War, 55; and senate reapportionment in 1981, 114–15; as Texas citizens, 50; in Texas House of Representatives, 100; and Texas population demographics, 201; twentieth-century electoral success of, 68; voting discrimination against, 62–63; and Voting Rights Act Section 5, 96–97
Alabama, 71
Alford, John, 138
Alger, Bruce, 68, 78
Alito, Samuel, 157, 165–66
Allred, Colin, 188, 209
American Community Survey (ACS), 182–83
Anglos: absolute dominance of Democratic, 67–68; and change in Democratic demographics, 208–9; declining percentage of, 191–92; distrust of Hispanics, 47; and Texas population demographics, 202. *See also* non-Hispanic white voters
apportionment: defined, 4–6; under early constitutions, 46–49; gridlock in establishing, 63–65; malapportionment, 67, 73; patterns in, 65–67; of Texas House, 184; of Texas Senate, 184. *See also* districting; gerrymandering; redistricting
Arizona, citizen redistricting commissions in, 211
Armbrister, Ken, 146
Armstrong, Bob, 89, 90, 106
Asian Americans, 202
at-large elections, and discrimination against minorities, 63
Avery, Hank, 84
Avery v. Midland County (1968), 84

bacon-strip districts, 112
Baker v. Carr (1962), 28–29, 74, 76
Balderas v. Texas (2002), 137
Barnes, Ben, 90
Barrientos v. State (2003), 147
Bell, Chris, 150
Bexar County, 49, 51, 92–93, 94, 109
bipartisan commissions, 210–11
Bonilla, Henry, 152, 153
Brennan, William, 114
Brown, John R., 78
Buchmeyer, Jerry, 108
Bullock, Bob, 106, 107
burden of proof, 36–38
Bush, George H. W., 76, 81, 85
Bush, George P., 186
Bush, George W., 128, 131, 134
Bush v. Martin (1963), 76, 79–80, 81–82

California, citizen redistricting commissions in, 211
Calvert, Robert S., 89
Calvert, Robert W., 89
Cameron County, xxii–xxiii, 112
Canales, José T., 61
census litigation, 119
"citizen" base, 197
citizen data, in redistricting, 182–85

voter polarization, 41
voter restrictions, 62
voter suppression, 97
voter turnout, 200
voting discrimination, against African Americans and Hispanics, 62–63
Voting Rights Act (1965): amendment to Section 2, 95; and burden of proof in redistricting litigation, 38; and discrimination against ethnic and racial minorities, 31–36; redistricting guidelines under, xxi; Section 2, 113–14, 163, 183, 188; Section 4(b), 156; Section 5, 108, 116, 126, 147, 156–57, 160–62, 187; Sections 4 and 5 applied to Texas, 96–97; text of, 223–25
voting rights litigation: complexity of, 38–39; judicial partisanship's role in, 42–44; nature of, 39–42
Voting Tabulation Districts (VTDs), 13

Ward, John, 137
Warren, Earl, 29
Washington, Craig, 114
Weiser v. White (1975), 116
Wentworth, Jeff, 135, 211–12
Wesberry v. Sanders (1964), 74–75, 78
White, James, 203
White, Mark, 106–7
White v. Regester (1973), 90, 93–95, 100. See also *Graves v. Barnes* (1972)
White v. Weiser (1973), 98–99
Whitmire, John, 146, 147
Wilson, Ron, xvii, 143
women, political involvement of, 203–4
Wood, John H., 91
Wurzbach, Harry M., 61, 68

ABOUT THE AUTHOR

STEVE BICKERSTAFF WAS AN ATTORNEY who served the State of Texas as Parliamentarian of the State Senate, director of the State Office of Constitutional Research, and assistant attorney general. In 1980, he joined Bob Heath to found a private law firm that, with the addition of Martha Smiley the following year, became known as Bickerstaff, Heath, and Smiley. The firm grew to fifty attorneys. Steve left the law firm after 26 years. It exists now as Bickerstaff Heath Delgado Acosta LLP.

Among Steve's most prominent achievements as a private attorney were a judgment for the largest monetary recovery ever awarded against the State of Texas ($204 million in an environmental suit); a multi-year, multi-forum fight to make telecommunications competitive in Texas and other states; a judgment holding the State financially responsible for convicted felons housed in county jails; forty-two years representing public entities and officials in redistricting; and the fostering of an independent citizens' commission to draw electoral districts in Austin, Texas.

During much of this time, Steve was also an adjunct professor at the University of Texas School of Law teaching constitutional law and voting rights. He taught as a Fulbright Scholar in Germany, was a Rockefeller Scholar in Residence at the Villa Serbelloni in Bellagio, Italy, was part of a Carter Commission study of elections in China, and lectured at sixteen different universities in the UK, Scandinavia, and elsewhere in Europe.

Steve was on the governing board of several nonprofits, including Trustees for Alaska, McDonald Observatory, and West Texas Public Radio. He served on the National Council of the National Parks Conservation Association.

Steve has authored six books and at least twenty-four law review articles and chapters in law anthologies. Most of these writings are about election issues.

ABOUT THE EDITOR

C. ROBERT (BOB) HEATH CO-FOUNDED what was then the Bickerstaff Heath law firm in 1980. He continues to practice in that firm, which is now known as Bickerstaff Heath Delgado Acosta L.L.P. He graduated with a BA and JD from the University of Texas, after which he served as a law clerk to a federal district judge and as chair of the Texas Attorney General's Opinion Committee prior to founding the law firm. He has worked on redistricting matters in every decade since 1971 when he was in law school. He, often with Steve Bickerstaff, has represented the state and local jurisdictions in multiple major redistricting cases. He and his wife reside in Austin.